MAK PEACE WITH REALITY

Ordering Your Life in a Chaotic World

JERRY WHITE

NAVPRESS

Bringing Truth to Life
P.O. Box 35001, Colorado Springs, Colorado 80935

OUR GUARANTEE TO YOU

We believe so strongly in the message of our books that we are making this quality guarantee to you. If for any reason you are disappointed with the content of this book, return the title page to us with your name and address and we will refund to you the list price of the book. To help us serve you better, please briefly describe why you were disappointed. Mail your refund request to: NavPress, P.O. Box 35002, Colorado Springs, CO 80935.

The Navigators is an international Christian organization. Our mission is to reach, disciple, and equip people to know Christ and to make Him known through successive generations. We envision multitudes of diverse people in the United States and every other nation who have a passionate love for Christ, live a lifestyle of sharing Christ's love, and multiply spiritual laborers among those without Christ.

NavPress is the publishing ministry of The Navigators. NavPress publications help believers learn biblical truth and apply what they learn to their lives and ministries. Our mission is to stimulate spiritual formation among our readers.

Library of Congress Catalog Card Number: 2001052196
ISBN 1-57683-217-1

Cover design by Dan Jamison
Cover photo-collage: sky from PhotoSpin / ground by Paul and Lindamarie Ambrose, FPG
Creative Team: Don Simpson, Glynese Northam

Some of the anecdotal illustrations in this book are true to life and are included with the permission of the persons involved. All other illustrations are composites of real situations, and any resemblance to people living or dead is coincidental.

Unless otherwise identified, all Scripture quotations in this publication are taken from the HOLY BIBLE: NEW INTERNATIONAL VERSION® (NIV®). Copyright © 1973, 1978, 1984 by International Bible Society. Used by permission of Zondervan Publishing House. All rights reserved. Other versions used include the New American Standard Bible (NASB), © The Lockman Foundation 1960, 1962, 1963, 1968, 1971, 1972, 1973, 1975, 1977; The Message: New Testament with Psalms and Proverbs (MSG) by Eugene H. Peterson, copyright © 1993, 1994, 1995, used by permission of NavPress Publishing Group; The New Testament in Modern English (PH), J. B. Phillips Translator, © J. B. Phillips 1958, 1960, 1972, used by permission of Macmillan Publishing Company; The Living Bible (TLB), copyright © 1971, used by permission of Tyndale House Publishers, Inc., Wheaton, IL 60189, all rights reserved; The Holy Bible, English Standard Version (ESV). Copyright © 2000; 2001 by Crossway Bibles, a division of Good News publishers. Used by permission. All rights reserved; and the King James Version (KJV).

White, Jerry E., 1937-
    Making peace with reality : ordering your life in a chaotic world / Jerry White.
        p. cm.
    ISBN 1-57683-217-1
    1. Christian life. 2. Chaos (Christian theology) I. Title.
BV4509.5 .W4543 2002
248.4--dc21   2001052196

Printed in the United States of America

1 2 3 4 5 6 7 8 9 10 / 06 05 04 03 02

"In the context of the World Trade Center terrorism, what could be more timely than a book about making sense out of the chaos of 21st Century life? This is Jerry's best book yet! It is crisp and current. It is filled with a broad range of wisdom from many sources, all wonderfully synthesized through the grid of a man who must 'make peace with reality' every day in his role as director of the Navigator mission around the globe."
— *Chris and Alice Canlis,* owners,
Canlis Restaurant, Seattle, Washington

"For some forty years, I have admired the life and ministry of Jerry White. In many ways, this book is the personification of who Jerry is—a man of mission, purpose, peace, perseverance, and passion. Every reader will benefit from this book."
—*Paul A. Cedar,* D. Min., chairman, Mission America

"A general in the celestial armed forces of America takes us to biblical principles for terrestrial peace in daily living. Practical, personal, provocative points for finding peace and one's purpose."
—*Jim Gwinn,* president, CRISTA Ministries

"Jerry White's book *Making Peace with Reality* is something we all desperately need. It could be subtitled, 'Coping with Chaos.' I wish it had been written years ago. It is exceptionally interesting and practical. I highly recommend it. Buy it and keep it."
—*Lorne Sanny,* former president, The Navigators

CONTENTS

To my grandchildren

Michael David Gray
Jerad Wesley Birch
Daniel Louis Gray
Joshua Stephen Birch
Hannah Janelle Birch
Jamison Andrew Gray
Bryan Christopher Gray
Jordan Eugene Birch
Shelby Ruth Thompson
Audrey Ann Thompson
Zachary Cross Thompson

Who will live in the reality of future chaos, and who will influence their world with their lives

ACKNOWLEDGMENTS

No book or writing—or life—ever springs up without influences from many people and events. Nor do we live alone, suffer alone, or struggle alone. Nor do we hope alone. So this book has found its way from mind and heart to pages of print through the inputs of many people in my life.

My thinking on reality and chaos began not long after our son's murder in 1990. As Mary and I rebuilt our lives, we saw more clearly the reality that engulfed so many of our friends and loved ones. We more deeply "felt" with them the stirrings of confusion and anxiety seemingly ignited by events beyond their control.

I have watched my friend and mentor, former president of The Navigators, Lorne Sanny, face cancer. Three couples, friends of more than twenty years, and we have engaged in what we call a "covenant relationship." Stan and Lois Newell, Chris and Alice Canlis, and Doug and Kaylinn Hignell comforted and confronted me time and time again, practically and spiritually, as I nurtured the replanted roots of my life. I also saw them walk through valleys of reality and times of chaos, drawing on the resources of our group as well as their personal walks with God.

I observed our dear friends and coworkers Donald and Jeanie McGilchrist walk through devastating health issues—and keep going. Additionally, Donald has given me several suggestions on parts of this manuscript.

Greg Williams assisted me in several avenues of research. Marjie Barnes, my executive assistant, came to my rescue typing the various drafts.

To all these my heartfelt thanks.

Mary White, my wife and coauthor on many books, applied her creative editing skills, challenging my extraneous words and clarifying my communication to the nontechnically inclined. I tried, unsuccessfully, to enlist her as coauthor. With her presence and love, the reality of the chaos of life became bearable. In fact, it became a deep pleasure of walking together and discovering new insights into ourselves, God, and the world. I cannot help but think that I am the stimulator of much of our chaos . . . and I thank her for standing by me in those many paths we have walked.

JERRY WHITE
Colorado Springs

THE REALITY OF CHAOS

In April of 1990 our son, Stephen, was brutally murdered. The event turned our lives upside down. Our beliefs have been challenged. Our emotions, put on a roller coaster. Our lives will never be the same.

But this is not a book to tell the story of our grief. Rather, the great loss we experienced caused us to reexamine what we believe, how we live—and why we live. It drew us into a world of chaos the depth of which we had never experienced. It brought us in contact with many people who were crushed by the events of life. But above all, we began to rebuild life in a more focused and purposeful manner.

My wife, Mary, and I are the first to confess that we don't have answers to all the troubling questions of life. But we have learned some crucial lessons about dealing with harsh reality, and we desire to thoughtfully communicate the exciting possibility of a life without regret—a life that rings true—not a theoretical picture of perfect living that ultimately discourages even the most serious seeker of truth. Life is lived in the trenches—down where battles are fought—and won or lost there. Just as military recruiting posters do not always show the grief and dirt of war, so most pictures of life and marriage do not always show the struggles and strains of reality. Even when we see or read about difficulties or struggles, we still picture in our minds an ideal future. Yet we want to look with reality at our humanness. The issues we face—failure, financial challenges, disappointments, marital stress, divorce, conflicts, family problems, health issues, discouragements—all are a part of reality.

This book has been forty years in the making. It has been forged in the fires of growth and failure as Mary and I have struggled to meet the increasing demands of career and family while at the same time trying to have a positive, spiritual influence on the people around us. However, my earliest notes for this specific writing go back to 1993 while I was still trying to recover emotionally from Steve's death.

In the meantime, the pace of change in the world has increased dramatically, with no sign that a respite will ever come. I have seen people increasingly immobilized by life's demands that come faster and faster.

This pace of life is not restricted to American or Western society. As I travel extensively in my work with the worldwide missionary organization The Navigators, I see the impact of chaos invading even the remote parts of the world. Tribal wars, increasing poverty, AIDS, economic disasters, and corruption bring a distinct type of chaos to the people of the less-developed world. At the same time they are impacted by television and other media that make them acutely aware of their plight. In the more technologically developed (not necessarily advanced!) countries, the genesis of the chaos is more related to disintegrating families, changing work patterns, and new economies. All over the world, stability and security are tenuous and fragile.

I invite you to walk with me in making peace with reality.

CHAPTER 1

A DANGEROUS INTROSPECTION

T minus 2 hours and counting

The majestic Atlas missile sat on its launch pad at Cape Canaveral with the early afternoon sun glinting off its shiny surface. The final fueling of the super-cold liquid oxygen was beginning. The shiny surface soon became crusted with frost as the frigid fuel met the Florida humidity.

In Central Control I sat at a console monitoring the progress of the many elements of the Atlantic Missile Range as they geared up to track and analyze the flight of this new rocket. It was a heady job for a twenty-three-year-old first lieutenant in the Air Force—especially for one who came from a very simple, lower-middle-class home. Having spent my first nine years in a small farm town—Garden City, Iowa, with a population of one hundred people—never in my wildest dreams had I envisioned being a mission controller in America's burgeoning space program.

T minus 1 hour and 38 minutes and counting

Tracking planes lifted off the runway at Ascension Island to record the reentry and splash down of the nose cone. Ships already on station waited to record the vital last minutes of the flight.

T minus 1 hour and 26 minutes—and holding
A problem developed with the preliminary checks of the internal guidance system. Engineers worked frantically to fix it. Thirty minutes went by. Still no resolution. Reports came in from the tracking aircraft on their available loiter time, giving their fuel levels. Soon they would have to return to their station to refuel.

T minus 1 hour and 26 minutes and counting!
The problem was finally fixed. Everyone breathed a sigh of relief. Each radar station along the Grand Bahama Islands down the range from Cape Canaveral reported their status. Grand Bahama Island experienced difficulties with their tracking radar. They assured me it would be ready by launch time.

T minus 43 minutes—and holding
A late-afternoon thunderstorm moved through. The winds were too high for launch. Topping off the fuel was delayed. Other tests were now being pushed later into the night. I received calls from the test directors. How quickly could we "turn around" after the launch? Why couldn't we do it faster?

The storm moved through. After a twenty-eight-minute hold, the count resumed. The sun slipped lower on the horizon.

T minus 30 minutes and counting
The fuel was topped off. The gantry began its slow retraction. Range safety officers checked all their systems. Charts showing the boundaries of safe flight were mounted. All tracking stations showed green. All aircraft and ships were in place.

T minus 10 minutes and holding
This was a "planned" hold for final checks. All reported okay. Count resumed.

Five, four, three, two, one. Ignition!

Engines ignited and thousands of gallons of water poured onto the concrete pad to keep it from being destroyed by the intense flame. The steam billowed around the base of the missile as it came to full power, straining against the hold-down clamps. Then, as the clamps released, the mighty Atlas slowly lifted into the air like a broom being balanced on a giant's finger. As it gained speed, it tilted southeastward toward its target.

In the range safety area several officers tracked the flight. At T plus 70 seconds, the missile veered to the south. Tracking telescopes saw a faulty flame in one of the small nozzles on the side of the great Atlas. The guidance system desperately tried to adjust and correct the path. Sweat beaded on the brow of the senior range safety officer. The pens on the tracking board showed the missile nearing the "destruct" boundary. The safety officer lifted the red cap of the destruct switch. At T plus 2 minutes the missile path intersected the destruct line. He flicked the switch and an explosive charge ripped the fuel tanks open. The night filled with a giant explosion as the missile burned and tumbled harmlessly into the Atlantic Ocean.

At Central Control we all sensed the disappointment—yet were also elated by the challenge of the future. All the data would be analyzed. Another test would be held. Success would come.

Meanwhile, the planes returned to station. Other tests began—on into the night. The work never stopped.

As I wrapped up my duties and got into the car for the thirty-minute drive home to Patrick Air Force Base, it was already 8:00 P.M. I walked in the house where Mary waited with dinner, having seen the explosion from our front yard. Our eighteen-month-old son, Stephen, was already in bed. He had been sleeping that morning when I left for work.

Together we sensed both the excitement of the times and our involvement as small players in this new frontier. Yet we also experienced a growing frustration in our lives and marriage. If it had just been work, that would have been understandable. But we realized the frustration went beyond work. It was because of our chaotic lifestyle.

We were involved in so many things. Mary worked for Pan American Airways to bring in some extra money that we erroneously thought we needed. We taught classes in the Base Chapel and led the chapel youth program. I sang in a choral society. I was part of a public speaking team for the Air Force Missile Test Center. I played sports. We hosted groups in our home. Our lifestyle was hectic, at best. I felt driven to activity and to achievement. The job was exciting. Life was exciting. There was so much to do. But Mary began to have a growing anger and frustration. She felt neglected. I gave little help in the home. I was oblivious to what was happening in our marriage and family.

Near the end of these two years, I became ill with exhaustion at the ripe old age of twenty-four! Then our second child, Katherine, was born just as astronaut John Glenn and Vice President Lyndon Johnson were driving by the front of the hospital after Glenn's historic first orbital flight. The pressures increased.

The space program excitement was at a fever pitch. A moon flight was next. But personally, Mary and I were ready to hit the panic button. It seemed that the excitement and importance of the task justified my hectic lifestyle. But that was a poor excuse. We felt trapped—on a treadmill from which we could not escape.

We vowed to make drastic adjustments in how we were living. But it was a long process to escape the drug of hyperactivity, of chaos.

Many of us know our lives are too busy, too occupied with activity, too frantic in pace. The pursuits that fill our time are not bad. They are worthwhile, good activities. They help people. They actually give us a sense of contribution and even a sense of fulfillment.

Our problem is one of chaos. Chaos is "a state in which chance is supreme; a state of utter confusion. This implies a wanting in order, sequence, organization, or predictable operation, causing things to be completely confused or disordered."[1]

Though we may not be in "utter confusion," we still experience chaos. However, many of us find it difficult to admit that we feel like this. Varying degrees of chaos exist in our lives. Some of us actually enjoy the feeling. We consider the activity as a sign of accomplishment.

In marriage one partner can be perfectly content with a high degree of activity while the other is paralyzed by it. We often encountered this in our marriage. I have a much greater tolerance—even enjoyment—of chaos than Mary has. In those early days, I was exhilarated. Mary was exhausted. I was energized. Mary was desperate. And that difference caused conflict between us.

In time, even those who are most tolerant of chaos begin to lose perspective, energy, and focus. We tire of the unpredictability and disorder. We long for tranquility and quietness. But life goes on with little change.

Then another issue begins to surface. Time. Not the use of time, but how much time is left in our lives. All of us come to a point when the thought strikes us, *There is not much time left. Life is passing me by.*

This can happen at any age. Although younger people are less likely to feel this desperation, they still sense panic at failing to reach the dreams they set out to fulfill. There is a hurry to do and to accomplish, increasing further the feeling of chaos, especially when we realize we cannot control our future in a rapidly changing world.

As we age, the feelings grow more acute:

✹ Have I achieved something?
✹ Did I do right by my family?
✹ Was it all worthwhile?
✹ Why don't I feel a sense of peace and accomplishment?

The words on an old clock in Winchester Cathedral express the feelings of many:

> *When as a child I laughed and wept, Time crept.*
> *When as a youth I waxed more bold, Time strolled.*
> *When I became a full-grown man, Time ran.*
> *When older still I daily grew, Time flew.*
> *Soon I shall find, in passing on, Time gone.*
> *Oh Christ! wilt Thou have saved me then?*
> *Amen.*

Our problem goes deeper. It is the sense that time was not used well. We experience the empty feeling of having wasted our life energy. We cannot change the past. It is gone, leaving only memories and a legacy for the present.

The great inventor Charles Kettering once wisely commented, "My interest is in the future because I am going to spend the rest of my life there." We can change only our direction for the future. The past teaches us, but it must not determine our future. Current decisions determine our future. This goes far beyond a "pull yourself up by your own bootstraps" philosophy. It is a conviction that God will bless good decisions that lead to deep inner fulfillment.

But here we encounter a major problem. Most of us are so busy attempting to keep life together that we cannot stop and think about where we are going. And if we did, would we like what we see?

We go, and keep on going,
Until the object of the game,
Seems to be
To go and keep on going.

We do, and keep on doing,
Until we do
Without knowing— without feeling.
Is there no time to stop and reflect?
Is there no time to stop?
Is there no time?

If we stopped, would we keep on going?
If we reflected, would we keep doing
What we do?

For what we have done
And where we have gone
Is dissolved into oblivion
Or strung on the meaningless chain
Of half-remembered this and that
If there is no reflection.

In all our doing have we done anything?
In all our going have we been anywhere?

Author unknown

Being an activist with what many would call a driven personality, I have needed to stop and regroup several times in
my life. No matter how much trimming I do at one point in
time, I soon find myself reverting to old habits, old ways of
thinking, and an increased pace. I need to do a major review
of my life and pace about every five years—with an annual
checkup and tune up.

When I do not do this, what happens? My family suffers.

They pay the price for my unexamined life. This is especially true for our children. They have no choice. They cannot escape. They are "stuck" with those of us who live lives that are too busy. The years pass so quickly. How I wish I could buy back some of those years when my children were small and I chose to be too busy.

This chaotic malady doesn't affect only high-flying executives or people in demanding professional careers. Those with forty-hour weeks and less-pressured jobs can fill their lives with recreation, hobbies, and other activities that keep them incredibly busy. Wives (both "stay-at-home" and "go-out-to-work" wives) create for themselves the same lifestyle panic as they spend hours transporting their children to sports, engaging in their social events, and trying to meet the incredible expectations of everyone around them.

Single mothers and fathers find themselves in an even more intensive activity cycle as they try to balance their work, family, social life (if they have time for one), and financial demands. The world does not stop to wait for them.

OUR CHAOTIC LIFESTYLES

I rarely talk with anyone who is not too busy. With the possible exception of the elderly, everyone has more to do than time in which to do it. In most cases, we choose this busy life. We are not forced into it, except by the expectation of our peers and the society in which we live. We want to enrich our children's lives so we schedule soccer, basketball, music lessons, social activities, church activities, home schooling, parties. Then we include the invasion of television, electronic games, the Internet, and CDs. They all add to our already complicated schedules and they come with good intent. We are trying to help our children, not harm them. Yet, almost as a drug-addicted mother impacts her newborn, we infect our children with a diet of activities, hurry, and packed schedules.

Are we making their lives more chaotic than they need to be?

In many families both husband and wife work. Even if the jobs are not the demanding sixty-hour-a-week kind, the pressures of the schedule are immense and intense. Many work out of necessity to provide private school tuitions, college educations, a house. I would not presume to judge those who choose to be a two-income family or to have a demanding career path, but I do want to emphasize the stress and pressure these place on a family. It simply adds to the chaos.

Church involvement, other spiritual activities, or community responsibilities add to an already demanding schedule. This explains why people are slow to volunteer for church and community needs.

The Chaos of the Inner Life

Chaos comes not only from the external influences of technology and schedules, but also from what takes place inside our minds and hearts. We wrestle with issues like restlessness, dissatisfaction, failure, spiritual emptiness, worry, and anxiety.

Other areas of the inner life, such as anger, depression, excessive ambition, or jealousy build the chaotic storm within us. At times they make the external chaos seem minor.

The chapters that follow deal with these ideas in more detail. So get a cup of your favorite drink, relax, and let yourself think about the issues of your own life direction. Perhaps you should fasten your seat belt too, because I predict there will be some rough roads as you allow yourself to think realistically about some of the deeper issues of your life—and the chaos that surrounds you. If you feel no chaos, you can close this book now. You have arrived. Or have you?

CHAPTER 2

A CHAOTIC WORLD,
A CHANGING WORLD

Do you remember when automobile odometers only registered up to 99,999.9 miles? I remember watching for this momentous occasion in one of my cars. For about a week ahead I carefully watched the odometer as it painstakingly climbed to that magic mark. I watched as it finally turned over from 99,999.9 to 00,000.0. Somehow I expected fireworks or some celebration. But everything just went on like the boring miles that preceded it. Nothing fell apart. The engine still ran. Nothing exploded. I didn't have to get a newer car, as much as I would have liked to. There was no change.

However, there had been considerable change, wear, and tear since the odometer began its circular trek from zero. Rust marks appeared. The exterior shine was dulled. Internal parts wore out and needed to be replaced. Automobile styles changed. Newer models raced by, with speed, efficiency, and electronic gadgets purportedly making them "newer and better." Nothing changed in the moment my odometer turned. But over the life of the car, much had changed.

As the year 2000 dawned on our Western calendar, little changed except the "time-o-meter" signaling a new millennium. The only noticeable effect was the hyped concern over the Y2K bug, creating a brief Y2K industry. The millennium was largely unnoticed in most of the underdeveloped world. Y2K came and went with a whisper, not a shout.

However, the changes in the past century have not been a whisper. They have been thunderclaps. Although one's eyes are always limited by the scope of one's lifetime, it does appear that the speed and impact of changes in the twentieth century are unprecedented in history. The momentous changes of past millennia were discoveries like fire, the wheel, and the production of iron and metal compounds, gunpowder, and firearms. These changes deeply influenced the daily lives of ordinary people and the defense of nations.

Many other significant discoveries and inventions—such as numbers and counting systems, mapping the earth, calendars, an accurate clock, the compass, the measurement of gravity, and the telescope and its associated astronomy—often had little immediate effect on ordinary people—or even nations. They were, however, foundational to later developments.

All of us have the sense that the world around us is changing too fast. The very word *change* has become so commonplace and hackneyed that it has almost lost its meaning. Yet change affects us deeply, both internally and externally.

With the turn of the calendar and the passing of birthdays, we sense the shortening of time in our lives. We question the importance of how we have spent our time in the past:

✖ "Did I do okay?"

✖ "Was I a good parent?"

✖ "What should I do now to make life more meaningful?"

These questions and feelings are compounded by the sense of living chaotic lives. We are too busy. We lead splintered lives with splintered families and activities. The whole of life for everyone seems to be in chaos. The acceleration of the speed of life, our constant accessibility by e-mail and cell phones, the pressures to perform and succeed and still do the "right" things for our children—these all contribute to a persistent angst, this feeling of being possessed by the urgency and demands of chaos.

How can we make sense out of this chaos? How do we cope with the complexities we encounter daily? The core question of this book is

> How do I order my life in the midst of the chaos in society and in my personal life?

To adequately answer this question, it is important to understand our recent history—how we got to where we are today. We wish to be focused on the present and the future, not stuck in the past. The past *teaches* but does not *determine*. You make the decisions that, in God's grace, set the future. We all live on borrowed time, by God's clock. Borrowed time is time that we do not own or control.

> *Teach us to number our days aright, that we might gain a heart of wisdom.*
> Psalm 90:12

A VIEW OF THE PAST
Ralph Waldo Emerson wisely observed, "There is properly no history, only biography."[1] History is not a recording of dry dates and events. Rather, history records the meaningful stories of men and women who have discovered, invented, and accomplished. Some changed the course of history. Others improved the lives of millions of people. Still others left misery, suffering, and despair in their wake.

History
In their view of history, Jim Taylor and Watts Wacker propose that every five hundred years major changes occur that mark a significant alteration in culture and history.[2]

23

✖ The birth of Christianity (4 B.C. to A.D. 28)
✖ The fall of Rome (A.D. 476)
✖ The collapse of feudalism (approximately A.D. 1100)
✖ The rise of the Renaissance (approximately A.D. 1300–1500)

Taylor and Wacker believe that we are now at the beginning of another five-hundred-year delta. They call this the "chaos age" and posit "new rules for a chaos world."[3]

As we review the past five hundred years, we see that the great names of Copernicus, Kepler, Galileo (all key figures in my profession of astronautics), Descartes, Locke, da Vinci, and Shakespeare are known to most. These men broke out of a strict religious control of their views to a new freedom in science and thinking, leading to what we now know as humanism.[4] Corporations, as we know them today, did not exist for most of this time, and the nation-state had emerged only in embryonic form.

Taylor and Wacker emphasize that we are rapidly shifting from *reason-based* to *chaos-based* logic; we are seeing a splintering of social, political, and economic organization and a collapse of a producer-controlled consumer market. Thus, they conclude, "rational theory has been replaced by chaos theory . . . in chaos, you cannot do, you cannot plan, you cannot reason. In chaos you can only be."[5] Though their conclusion is somewhat poetic and extreme, it does give a strong sense of living in chaotic times. The authors also show the demise of family and family values. (They apply their research primarily to business, but the implications for individuals and families are immense.) With one-third of all marriages ending in divorce within seven years and another 15 percent within 14 years, 75 percent of our children are under new family structures.[6] Holding the family together is a constant fight against forces that would rip it apart.

We can predict certain futures by looking at the past. The

unknowns in such predictions are catastrophic events and breakthrough discoveries. Earthquakes and volcanoes have destroyed cities, virtually changing the course of a nation as well as the lives of millions of people. Even Old Faithful, the once-predictable geyser in Yellowstone National Park, was made unpredictable by a small earthquake. The eruption of Mount Pinatubo in the Philippines wiped out a city and an American Air Force Base, hastening the American military withdrawal. No one can predict these events. Each of the five-hundred-year deltas, as described by Taylor and Wacker, was interspersed with wars, plagues, and natural disasters. The main difference today is that we now have the power to create plagues and mass disasters. We now must depend upon human restraint against human madness.

In the first half of the twentieth century, the two World Wars drew the world closer and nearly tore it apart. No modern country was the same after these wars, which were fueled by greed, economic imperatives, and hunger for dominance and power. By 1950, the world was shaped by the two emerging superpowers, the United States and Russia. That bipolar political power struggle dominated the next forty years. In the last half of this century, the "regional" wars of Korea and Vietnam were flanked by hundreds of less publicized wars around the world. Dozens of nations gained their independence only to flounder economically and politically in their newfound freedom. The gap between rich and poor has widened, leaving the world in a tension of wondering when it will come apart at the seams.

Science and Technology
Some of the most profound and revolutionary changes have occurred in science. Technological and scientific discoveries frequently tilted the balance of power among nations in war, economics, and culture.

In the twentieth century, these key discoveries and inventions propelled us into the world of chaos we see today:

The invention of the internal combustion engine by Nikolaus Otto in Germany in 1876 forever changed our ability to apply power to labor-intensive tasks. The familiar names of Karl Benz, Gottlieb Daimler, and Rudolf Diesel still mark the industry. This was a natural step to cap the Industrial Revolution and the earlier use of the steam engine (invented in 1698).

The mass production of the automobile for the ordinary person changed the culture of our society in terms of mobility and community.

The use of antibiotics, embodied in the discovery of penicillin in 1928 by Sir Alexander Fleming, revolutionized medical care and significantly lengthened human life. In the Civil War, as many soldiers died from infected wounds as from immediate battle actions. This paved the way for the myriad antibiotics in use today. In one sense, penicillin is the symbol of the incredible pantheon of chemical cures (medicines) currently on the market.

Electricity has been foundational to most of the discoveries and technologies listed here. Today we cannot live without electric power. It fuels communications, industry, computers, and most of the conveniences in our homes—air conditioning, furnaces, refrigerators, washers, dryers, and small appliances. We are totally dependent on it.

The invention of the airplane and its incredibly rapid development changed the way wars are fought, made international travel commonplace, and generally destroyed the ability of a nation to live in total isolation. Along with communications technology, airplanes and air travel joined the nations of the world irreversibly, making an isolationist posture an impossibility.

Nuclear energy, riding on the landmark discoveries of Germans Otto Hahn and Fritz Strassman in 1939, gave the twentieth century the title "The Century of Physics." The detonation of the atomic bomb in Japan in 1945 placed the power to destroy ourselves in human hands. This event heralded the tenuous balance of power during the Cold War. Today the continued proliferation of nuclear weapons frightens millions of world citizens. As with most discoveries, nuclear energy can be used for good and for evil. With the future discovery of proper disposition of nuclear waste, the use of nuclear energy may solve the energy problems of a world rapidly using up its natural resources of oil, gas, and coal.

Communications technology, like travel, has revolutionized the way people interact over distance. From runners, carrier pigeons, early telegraph, and mail systems have emerged the mass communication technologies of telephone, radio, television, and the Internet. These inventions rode on the backs of earlier discoveries in materials, electricity, and electronics.

When I was a boy in Garden City, Iowa, my phone number was 9. We placed calls through "central." Today, ten-digit numbers, multiple lines in homes, and satellite networks for phone systems are the norm. This all happened in sixty short years.

Space programs and space technology fueled the electronic communications and defense industries. From the launch of the Russian satellite Sputnik on October 14, 1957, to the United States landing on the moon on July 20, 1969, satellites and ballistic missiles became a controlling technology of the last forty years. They revolutionized the face of war and the medium of communication. Satellites with highly accurate photography revolutionized intelligence gathering, weather prediction, and agricultural and global mapping. Satellites in geosynchronous orbits crowd that unique band at 22,300 miles above the equator. Thousands of satellites compete for space and broadcast frequencies. The Global Positioning System has made navigation and surveying a new science. Even a hiker can find his or her exact location with a hand-held device. The miniaturization of electronics and the development of new materials were significantly propelled by the space program. All these have become part and parcel of a wireless society.

Finally, we come to *computers and the information technology revolution*. In fifty years, computers have reduced in size and cost by orders of magnitude. The watch on your wrist holds as much computing power as existed in the world in 1950! If the same progress had been made in automobile technology as in computers, you could buy a Lexus for eight dollars and travel six hundred miles on a thimbleful of gas.[7]

We are all impacted by the onslaught of information in our lives: hundreds of television channels, faxes, cell phones, answering devices, voice-activated controls, electronic mail, the Internet, and much more. One can hardly call a company and get a live person without going through a maze of questions and responding to choices by voice or touch-tone buttons.

I remember working on my Ph.D. dissertation on the Air Force Academy's central computer in 1969. I used the entire computer system all night long to conduct one major calculation. The computer itself filled a large room. Today I could do the same problem on my laptop in seconds, or at most, minutes. It is this computing speed and power that enable our modern communications, our frontline scientific research, our business systems, and our devices of war. Again, we have become irretrievably dependent. And this is just the beginning.

Economics, Business, and Politics

Because of my background, it is far easier for me to outline the scientific events of the past and the scientific changes portending the future. The world of economics and business is much less defined and traceable by events—or even by people. Whereas scientific and technological breakthroughs tip the scales of war and ruling powers, economics affect the ordinary person daily. Money, food, shelter, and safety are their primary concerns.

With the collapse of feudalism and the later waning of the Renaissance, the Industrial Revolution transformed the production and delivery of goods and services. While agriculture still remained the primary occupation in most of the world, industry and corporations began to emerge and dominate. The flight from rural to urban living changed the face of family, community, and culture. The driving forces were mass production, efficient transportation systems, new machinery, and specialization in manufacturing. Especially, new ways of leveraging capital enabled this revolution. This ushered in a new view of economics.

Factors in the chain of time and events that positioned today's economics and politics are numerous and often convoluted. Yet a few cry out for our attention:

Capitalism, socialism, and communism. The twentieth century was dominated by maturing capitalism with its focus on individualism and free-market forces governed by supply and demand—with little government intervention. Capitalism is undergirded by private enterprise and a banking system that provides large sums of money for borrowing. Inherent in capitalism is the right to own property.

The opponent to capitalism was socialism. Although the roots of socialism can be traced to Plato and even the New Testament, modern socialism is a product of the French Revolution (1789-1793) and the Industrial Revolution in England (the term was first used in 1827 in an English journal). Socialism is rooted in the conflict between property owners and workers. Equality, social justice, and individual freedom are central themes. Socialists oppose private ownership and espouse public or state ownership.

In the mid-nineteenth century, Marx and Engels wrote the *Communist Manifesto*, which stimulated the primary form of socialism that dominated the last half of the twentieth century as it evolved into communism.

The more moderate forms of socialism reside in western Europe—in nations such as Sweden, Britain, France, and Germany. In reality, there are no truly capitalistic nations nor are there any successful extreme socialist nations. Rather, they blend along a spectrum, with the United States carrying the banner as the most capitalistic. Even here, government intervention in monetary systems, monopolies, and welfare arguably undermine pure capitalistic goals.

The gross failure of communism in the 1980s now leaves only the tug-of-war between diluted forms of capitalism and socialism. But these forms are in no way independent of the pervasive issues of globalization, international monetary policies, and democratization.

World trade and globalization. World trade dates back to the Hebrew, Egyptian, Arabian, and Asian caravans. In the time of Christ and the early Christian church, the Roman Empire was tied together by about fifty thousand miles of roads—and thus, by the trade of goods within the empire. Later, the importing of natural resources was a foundation of the great colonial powers and colonial expansion.

Today no nation can prosper without import and export trade. Tariffs and laws either inhibit or encourage such trade. Punishment of nations is meted out by trade barriers and restrictions—for example, those enforced against Cuba, China, and Iraq.

We are now at the cusp of a major revolution in what is loosely referred to as "globalization." This term is broader than "world trade." It speaks of businesses that span nations and boundaries. Automobiles are composed of parts manufactured in many countries. Software is developed around the clock with developers in Europe passing their work to the United States and then to India and back to Europe, tripling the speed of production. Manufacturing goes where labor is the cheapest. And money and financial markets know no boundaries with the instant computer trading now present around the world.

Certainly national economies exist, but no robust economy will exist without globalization. We now live in a truly global economy.

The Great Depression. The twentieth century was deeply marked by the U.S. stock market crash of 1929 and the economic depression of the 1930s. These events left a legacy of underlying fear of financial collapse, the intrusiveness of government controls, and policies controlling the stock market and currencies. The Depression marked at least two generations with fear and frugality. On the other hand, those of us growing up in the fifties and beyond have been largely untouched by severe economic crises. We are now so used to prosperity and a "see it, buy it" mentality that we cannot imagine anything else.

Democratization. The United Nations has 183 members (and counting!). In the last two decades, the majority of these countries have become democratic, at least in name.[8] No longer do monarchs, despots, or ruling classes govern the majority of nations. Yet many of those nations claiming to be democratic are fraught with corruption and tribal preferences.

Alonzo McDonald, a business executive and former U.S. ambassador and assistant to the U.S. president, comments, "It is a strange irony, . . . that although such a high proportion of the world's citizens have never before had the opportunity to express their will through political elections, how few long-standing democracies now exercise that privilege."[9] Whether or not democracy is the best form of government for all nations, the West is bent on making democracy a requirement for financial aid. Thus, democratization is almost a type of financial or global control. Only time will tell as to the efficacy of such a policy.

The Onset (Edge) of Chaos

All this history sets the stage for what is happening now. But does the past matter? Think of sitting in your car at a stop sign, waiting to enter a fast, busy highway. As you see oncoming cars, your mind and eyes quickly calculate the speed and make a decision on how much time you have to enter the highway. To do this, your eyes and mind *must* see the oncoming car at several points over a period of time to calculate the speed.

Similarly, we need to see the pace of the past to determine if today's pace and events are truly faster and more intense. Even though our older generations lament the increased pace of their lives and long for the quieter days of the past (smoothed over by selective memories and the passage of time), we cannot stop progress. Life does seem to be accelerating. In Daryl Conner's book *Leading at the Edge of Chaos*, he observes: "Chaos is entered into where significant disruptions pile up on people long after they have exceeded their available adaptation resources."[10] He expresses our fear of change and excessive chaos:

> What formerly excited and inspired us has begun to threaten, terrify and immobilize. The world is inundated with disruptions: unforeseen dangers, unanticipated opportunities, unmet expectations, alarming new statistics, startling twists of fate, shocking innovations, unheralded improvements, unrealistic requirements, overwhelming demands, contradictory directives, staggering liabilities, astonishing results, sudden strokes of luck and more. At every turn there is something that we didn't see coming. Some of life's surprises are good and some are bad, but we seem to be constantly contending with *more than we bargained for or less than we think we need.* (Emphasis mine.)[11]

In his book *Margin,* futurist and physician Richard Swenson demonstrates the acceleration of change and inundating information by a series of charts showing exponential growth in recent years. "Exponential" relates to the increasingly steep curve in the plotting of data. We have personally experienced most of these, such as the increase in pieces of mail (from 25 billion in 1940 to 175 billion and counting) and new books published annually (about 10,000 from 1900–1940, now 50,000). The years 1960–2000 experienced the greatest increase in such areas as gross national product, IRS collections, federal debt, bankruptcies, and especially health-care costs.[12]

In terms of information and communication, the science fiction of the 1960s is reality now. We are inundated with information, demands on our minds and time, the invasion of a wired society, and an environment where computers are as common to children as pencils were to our parents.

We live in a different world—one that is accelerating with change and fraught with uncertainty. We cannot alter its march. It is our reality. In all likelihood it will continue. Also, we should note that change is not synonymous with progress. Change, in and of itself, can lead to progress or disaster. It can enhance or tear down. We want the change that leads to progress.

In the magazine *The Futurist,* science writer James Gleick tells us that we are living faster and faster: "We do feel that we are more time-driven and time-pressed than ever before." He comments,

> Technology has conditioned us to expect instant results. Internet purchases arrive by the next-day delivery ... faxes, E-mails and cell phones make it possible—and increasingly obligatory—for people to work faster ... up tempo living has turned people into multi-taskers—eating while driving, writing an E-mail while talking on the phone or skimming dozens of television programs on split screens.[13]

Gleick concludes with the perceptive statement, "Neither technology nor efficiency can acquire more time for you, because time is not a thing that you have lost. It is not a thing that you have ever had. It is what you live in. You can drift or swim, and it will carry you along either way."[14]

Time is our most perishable resource. We wish to use it wisely—to invest it, to enjoy it, to make it our friend. Panic, busyness, frustration, fear, and uncertainty all spoil the time we have and the time we anticipate. Though we live in the present, we must somehow anticipate the future. That is difficult, if not impossible, to do with any degree of accuracy beyond a few months or years.

THE FUTURE

With the turn of the "calendar-o-meter" to January 1, 2000, many magazines and newspapers revisited the predictions and futurists of the past. The *Wall Street Journal* was one of the most interesting. Let's compare some predictions for 2000 with today's reality—and then (perhaps foolishly) look at some predictions for the next decades.[15]

✹ 1893: "Three hours will constitute a long day's work by the end of the next century. And this work will literally furnish infinitely more of the benefits of civilization and the comforts of life than 16 hours' slavish toil will today."[16]

✹ 1982: "There will be shorter work weeks . . . 25 hours by 2000. Flexible schedules will be the rule, with two or three people sharing a job and arranging their shifts."[17]

> *The reality:* For most, forty hours a week is the minimum, with overtime common in a labor-scarce society. Professionals work fifty to sixty hours a week. In many cases, both for necessity and desire, both husband and wife work in the marketplace, still struggling to make ends meet.

✖ 1975: "The average man will live to be 100."[18]

> *The reality:* Not quite. Life spans for males are approaching seventy-seven years in the United States.

✖ 1900: "War as an institution will be as obsolete as gladiators in the year 2000 . . . War is too wasteful, as well as too imbeciley uncivilized, to survive the century."[19]

> *The reality:* The world was engulfed in two major wars; the United States, in two others. Now, at this writing, over thirty wars rage on.

✖ 1967: "[It is] unlikely that everyone will have his own computer any time soon." The RCA forecast was that the U.S. would have 220,000 computers by . . . 2000.[20]

> *The reality:* Today there are fifty million computers and increasing. Computers in homes have become common—many homes have more than one.

To be fair, there were also some very good predictions: air travel, the reunification of Germany, increased opportunities for women, a postindustrial society, and computer-connected homes and offices (1965). Whatever the fear or the danger, we must look ahead.

Only as we envision the future can we discern the preparation and adjustments we need to make in the present. The uncertainty of the future can make it somewhat frightening but, believing God is still in control, we can move forward with confidence that we will adjust, adapt, and even prosper—spiritually and personally. I do not believe in scare tactics or dire predictions of impending doom—even when there are some ominous developments on the horizon.

In spite of a phenomenal failure rate, futurists continue to predict progress and catastrophes. The authors of *The 500-Year Delta* predict that in the five hundred weeks after their book was written (about 2007):

✖ China will have the largest economy.

✖ On-line learning will have driven one-third of current four-year colleges and universities out of business.

✖ The pharmaceutical management of aging will have become a global mania.

✖ Children will regularly have sex before the age of ten.

✖ A competency test will determine the right to vote.

✖ There will be a holy war between Muslims and Christians.

✖ There will be a bio-accident that will jeopardize the future of the world.

Then in the next five hundred months (about 2039):

✖ There will be term limits on life based on each individual's ability to pay for his or her own care.

✖ Reproduction will be taxed, and each person will be limited to the ownership of one child.

✖ Life-form hatcheries will be one of the most important emerging industries globally, and the overriding philosophical question will be whether we are still the creatures of God's will in producing these new species.

✖ A nuclear bomb will have been set off by a terrorist organization.[21]

We may scoff at some of these seemingly bizarre predictions, yet we can see their possibility. I chose those that seemed to have the greatest likelihood.

The Futurist magazine steps forward again with its top ten predictions.[22] Among them are:

✖ The number of centenarians worldwide will increase from 135,000 today to 2.2 million by 2050.

- Tiny electronic microchips implanted in a person's forearm could transmit messages that control the heating and light systems of intelligence buildings.
- The twenty-first century could see widespread infertility and falling birth rates.
- Ninety percent of the world's six thousand languages could go extinct by 2100.
- Water scarcity could threaten one billion people by 2025.

These are all quite plausible. Yet they do not really set off many alarms in our chaos-sensitive systems. The greater impact on us as individuals and families will come from several trends that, connected with the recent past, are quite predictable. In my research I have identified trends in six areas (information technology, privacy, biogenetics, aging, jobs and careers, and the family) that will impact our personal lives, intensifying the chaos we feel. These trends affect us whether we want them to or not. They are out of our control, much like the weather.

Information Technology

Computers and electronic communications will continue to rapidly change and permeate every area of our lives. Computers will be as pervasive as the telephone. Shopping, medical records, banking, government inquiries, and most communications will be electronic. Computers and software will be everywhere. They will be a part of our way of life. They will do more, work faster, and cost less.

According to another *Wall Street Journal* article, "The Faith of the Futurist," "Soon single cable(s) will carry as much traffic as the entire American Internet infrastructure carried in one month in 1997."[23]

The future is in what David Gelernter, professor of computer science at Yale, calls "cyberbodies."

> Your whole electronic life is stored in a cyberbody ... walk
> up to any viewer (say a computer on your desk or at the
> supermarket), slip in your calling card and give your pass-
> word. The cyberbody itself tells the viewer what to do next
> ... your school and company, your car and self are all vehi-
> cles moving through time, and they will each leave a stream-
> shaped cyberbody (like an aircraft's contrail) behind them
> ... our institutional and private lives will be cyberbody-
> centric ... when you connect to your stream, you connect
> to a world in which your habits are well known.[24]

This is not theory. It is in the developmental phase. We have
instant access to information and connections—but we are
also instantly accessible. In one sense, we can never escape.

Cell phones, e-mail, the Internet, and "smart" homes are
just the threshold of a cyber-future. The wild card is the pen-
etration and pollution of such systems by rogue computer
viruses. But even these will be dealt with. Today's irritants and
insurmountable problems are simply bumps on the road—
which will be overcome. To think otherwise would deny our
electronic history.

Privacy

With the onslaught of computers and communication
advances comes the real threat of decreasing privacy. While
some believed bar codes were the "mark of the beast" from
biblical prophecy, we experience other increasing threats to
privacy and freedom as we buy and sell. As the *Wall Street
Journal* January 2000 issue said,

> It's 2005, and within hours of booking a flight to Las Vegas on-
> line, your E-mail box is spilling over with messages from
> hotels offering room specials. Knowing you subscribe to an
> on-line newsletter for heart-bypass patients, one whole hotel

> trumpets its in-room defibrillators. A nearby casino, tipped
> off that you recently have surfed pornography web sites,
> touts lap dancing ... The car rental agency rejects you after a
> database records you've had a recent accident.[25]

The *Wall Street Journal* article goes on to describe the loss of privacy in the digital world. It refers to insurance companies having your genetic profile (which reveals susceptibility to disease) and employers seeking out your political opinions and much more. A *Wall Street Journal*/NBC poll showed a loss of privacy was the number-one concern for the twenty-first century.

At the same time, an entirely new industry of privacy protection methods in software is springing up. The Better Business Bureau of Arlington, Virginia, recently announced an "on-line privacy seal," which companies would receive if they subscribed to specific privacy guidelines. Dr. Alan Westin, emeritus professor of law at Columbia and a long-time examiner of privacy issues, believes that "managing our privacy will become our everyday activity in the 21st century and beyond, requiring as much energy and thought as managing finances has in the 20th century."[26]

However, all of this costs money . . . and the less informed or the poor may well suffer incursions while the affluent protect themselves. Look for an increase of government intervention in this arena.

Just imagine the chaos in your mind and life if you no longer could protect your privacy. The protection of privacy is a huge issue—and a source of increasing chaos.

Biogenetics

The twentieth century has been called "The Age of Physics." The twenty-first century is already being titled "The Age of Biology." With the unveiling of the Human Genome Project's complete mapping of DNA, the future of genetic cures and manipulation has become reality. This will become one of the great ethical battlegrounds of the future. While we desperately wish for a cure for cancer, diabetes, multiple sclerosis, and so many other killers, we fear the other side—genetic selection of babies, fetal harvesting, and cloning. Can we have one without the other?

The *Wall Street Journal* called genetic engineering "the wild card of the new millennium," stating that "manipulation of genes could change the innate capacity for good and evil that has marked mankind through all the ages."[27]

We shall see.

Aging

Forever Young is the title of a popular movie. But no one is. We all age—some gracefully, some fighting it all the way. We all want the wisdom of age, the energy of youth, and the health of a twenty-five-year-old. A brief visit to almost any nursing home shatters any glamorization of aging.

In America, in contrast to Africa and Asia, the elderly are not highly respected. The younger generation envies and seeks after the older generation's power and affluence, perceiving that their elders have the good jobs and the money. But if you listen to the older generation, they tell another story. In our country, most men over fifty find it difficult to land a good job commensurate with their training and experience. They feel "run over" by the "young turks." They fear poverty and nursing homes.

The reality is that we are an aging nation. Though the less-developed countries, buffeted by AIDS and poor health care, abound in young people, the Western world's population is tilting toward people living longer. Life expectancy in the United States was 46 years in 1941 and 77 years in 2000. The next fifty years will see an increase of 300 percent of people between 65 and 84 years of age, and of those over 85,

600 percent—and a 1,600-percent increase of those over 100!

"The gray wave" is in full swing in America, gaining more power all the time. Thus, any politician who tampers with Social Security does so at great peril. We already see numerous implications of this gray trend.

✖ Health care will be in continual crises. People who reach sixty-five will still be caring for *their* parents.

✖ Diet and exercise programs and facilities are a major industry. Wellness programs and holistic ministries will be commonplace.

✖ The widening gap between rich and poor will adversely impact the elderly poor.

Jobs and Careers

When one enters college and selects a major, career possibilities will have drastically changed by graduation. In my father's generation a person had one career and two jobs. In my generation it was two careers and three to five jobs. In my children's generation it will be three to five careers and ten to fifteen jobs.

No longer does one join a prestigious company and stay there for a lifetime. That experience will join outdoor toilets and hand-cranked telephones in nostalgic history books. New companies and careers are being birthed with regularity. My 1959 electrical engineering degree is about as useful as my appendix. Even my Ph.D. is hopelessly outdated—leaving me with reputation but little current skill in my field.

Continuing education and retraining will be the norm. Entire industries have collapsed. Security and loyalty in the marketplace are relics of the past. No retirement program is secure, with budgets and takeovers reshaping and eliminating them. Thus, job security is always tenuous. For the over-forty-five workers, this is especially frightening. For the younger workers, this is all they have ever known.

The Fractured Family and Disintegrating Values

This is a trend that has been decried by religious and social conservatives for the past quarter-century. Now it is reality.

According to Taylor and Wacker, "In 1960, the average child had one set of parents and two sets of grandparents. Today, the average child has two-and-a-half sets of parents and six sets of grandparents."[28] Single mothers give birth to 1.3 million babies every year. Abortions have become commonplace. Taylor and Wacker further remark, "The myth of family drives the political debate over family values. The reality is that 'families' are largely a status symbol today, a luxury for those who can keep them intact."[29]

The age of first sexual intercourse is decreasing for boys and girls. The data is about the same for Christian children. Pornography, violence, and immorality permeate the media. Divorce is so common as to hardly draw notice—except by the children whose lives are forever impacted.

Our increasingly secular and postmodern world in the West only propels us further down the road to a society with decreasing moral values. The external religious fervor of America has done little to reverse the trend. In thirty years, America has experienced the increase of violent crime by 500 percent, while the population grew only about 40 percent.[30]

Social and moral standards continue to disintegrate, adding continued pressure to keep our families together. It will accelerate the chaos as declining values impact our children with divorces, drugs, shattered lives, and changing value systems.

BECOMING CHAOTIC

When we put all of these trends together, our lives are becoming more and more chaotic. We cannot escape their impact. Nor should we. Every generation has faced its challenges. We must now face ours.

CHAPTER 3

INTERPRETING CHAOS—WHERE DOES IT COME FROM?

IMAGINE LIFE AS A GAME IN WHICH YOU ARE JUGGLING FIVE BALLS IN THE AIR. YOU NAME THEM—WORK, FAMILY, HEALTH, FRIENDS, AND SPIRIT, AND YOU'RE KEEPING ALL THESE IN THE AIR. YOU WILL SOON UNDERSTAND THAT WORK IS A RUBBER BALL. IF YOU DROP IT, IT WILL BOUNCE BACK. BUT THE OTHER FOUR BALLS—FAMILY, HEALTH, FRIENDS, AND SPIRIT—ARE MADE OF GLASS. IF YOU DROP ONE OF THESE, THEY WILL BE IRREVOCABLY SCUFFED, MARKED, NICKED, DAMAGED, OR EVEN SHATTERED. THEY WILL NEVER BE THE SAME. UNDERSTAND THAT, AND STRIVE FOR BALANCE IN YOUR LIFE. YESTERDAY IS HISTORY, TOMORROW IS A MYSTERY, AND TODAY IS A GIFT. THAT'S WHY WE CALL IT ... THE PRESENT.
BRYAN DYSON, CEO, COCA-COLA ENTERPRISES

THE CURSE OF COMPLEXITY /
THE LONGING FOR SIMPLICITY

By most standards, Kevin was a successful man. When I met him his business was thriving, although often close to financial crisis. He was a tenacious, capable businessman, but changing markets for the product he manufactured and the materials he needed forced him to work long hours to keep turning a profit. His marriage suffered. Then he discovered he had cancer!

Suddenly, Kevin's chaotic life came to a standstill. Was it all worth it? Where was God? What should he do now? The business had to continue. But what about enjoying life? How should he use the money he had made?

He hit on an idea. He ordered a specially made sea-going yacht. He intended to enjoy some sailing. He anticipated spending leisure time away from business. He traveled to Paris to see the keel being laid. As he returned home, Kevin encountered someone next to him on the plane reading his Bible. I was that person. We started a long conversation. I shared my personal view of God. Kevin and his wife had watched a religious program that raised the same idea. He returned home wrestling with these ideas and shared them with his wife.

Kevin was a driven man. For what? Success, money, achievement, business, challenge? But was that what he was really seeking?

Kevin was a man whose life and business were in chaos. Where did this chaos come from? I'll finish Kevin's story later.

In the previous chapter, I reviewed many of the external chaotic forces influencing us. But that is only part of the picture. Let's backtrack a bit to discuss two concepts: chaos and complexity.

CHAOS THEORY

Chaos Theory was developed in the fields of mathematics and science to describe and understand seemingly irregular or erratic fluctuations in nature. Evidence of chaos is seen in the movement of weather, wave motion and fluids (such as the ocean), electrical currents and semi-conductors, and medical disorders (such as heart arrhythmias and epileptic seizures).

These systems appear to be unchartable, yet they do obey the laws God established. They are complicated with dynamics for which we simply do not possess the capability to measure and model.

The second major concept is *complexity.* Most of us relate *complexity* with the word *complicated.* That is not quite the meaning. Complex systems have many related parts that interact with each other in sometimes unknown ways. Consider ant colonies, the human brain, human cultures (or societies), and immune systems. An automobile is complicated in that it has so many interrelated parts, but it is predictable. Although we don't know when a part will break due to fatigue or wear, each part has a predictable function; thus, an automobile is not a classic complex system.

Complex systems often organize themselves into patterns and structures. Weather systems can be tracked in a narrow sense, but the complexity resides in the smaller interactions of cold and warm air, land and sea, mountains, heat from the sun, and moisture content—none of which can easily be analyzed. Complexity can then lead to chaos as the system becomes completely unpredictable.

While we were living in Florida, our home was only one hundred feet from the Atlantic Ocean. As a major hurricane battered us, we geared up to evacuate. Water in our back yard began rising. We listened to the weather forecasts, attempting to learn when the hurricane would arrive in force. Then, as in so many cases, it unpredictably veered, sparing us. That is a system in chaos.

Both Complexity Theory and Chaos Theory are being extensively used in business and science today.

The human issues surface when our lives become complex with unplanned and unpredictable events intersecting. These collisions lead to panic—and ultimately, chaos. An unplanned pregnancy, a child's illness, drop-in guests, the death of a loved one, job loss, conflicts, car accidents—these unexpected events trigger a complex set of actions and interactions, both internally and externally. When too many of these events intertwine in too short a time, we begin to panic. Soon our bodies respond with illness, depression, or anxiety.

The feeling of *not being in control* is the most difficult. Control is the one thing we want—and seemingly need— for our own stability and well-being. If we cannot control *all* the infringements on our lives, at least we want to control our responses to them. We want to manipulate and think our way through them. We want the sense of being in charge.

In my life, I want not only to be a controller but also a "fixer." One of my daughters said in exasperation, "Dad, forget it. You can't fix everything!" She was right. I must surrender the urge to control. I can acknowledge God's control over everything (what choice do I have?) but still feel that I can solve whatever problems come to me. This is arrogance. It is also a way of combating or enduring a sense of chaos.

As both complexity and chaos increase, we truly lose control. There is little we can do to stem the tide of change and the speed of change. That is where we find ourselves in contemporary culture. The external forces of change have overcome us.

In addition to incredible societal changes, other factors emerge:

- Troubled and broken marriages
- Demanding children
- Financial pressures
- Job and career disappointments
- Personal battles with lust, anger, or pride
- Purposelessness

King Solomon, who had everything his wealth could buy, grimly reflected:

In my opinion, nothing is worthwhile; everything is futile. For what does a man get for all his hard work?

Generations come and go but it makes no difference. The sun rises and sets and hurries around to rise again. The wind blows south and north, here and there, twisting back and forth, getting nowhere. The rivers run into the sea but the sea is never full, and the water returns again to the rivers, and flows again to the sea ... everything is unutterably weary and tiresome. No matter how much we see, we are never satisfied; no matter how much we hear, we are not content.

History merely repeats itself. Nothing is truly new; it has all been done or said before. What can you point to that is new? How do you know it didn't exist long ages ago? We don't remember what happened in those former times, and in the future generations no one will remember what we have done back here. (Ecclesiastes 1:2-11, TLB)

As chaos, complexity, and change batter us, we are tempted to give up—to despair of finding a way out. But there is a way out. God has given us tools to cope and a human spirit that can adjust. We have many reasons to hope.

Before we attempt to solve our problems, let's identify the sources of chaos.

EXTERNAL CHAOS

The entire previous chapter outlined the societal issues that contribute to chaos. One of our temptations is to "escape to the mountains," seeking a simpler life. I will discuss this approach near the end of this chapter.

Societal chaos pounds on us heavily, but some of the most dangerous external chaos emerges from sources that have little to do with rapid change in society and technology.

Self-Induced External Chaos

Many of us bring chaos into our lives by our *own* actions, decisions, and drives.

- Many marriage breakups are clearly self-induced. Insensitivity, infidelity, and inattention destroy many marriages. A refusal to seek help, to communicate, and to really work on our marriages sows the seeds of divorce.
- An abrasive, self-seeking personality creates conflict and relational problems that literally destroy relationships and personal peace. A failure to recognize the need for change and character development dooms us to self-induced chaos.
- Foolish financial mistakes put enormous pressures on many families. Easy credit, undisciplined buying, rampant materialism, and vices such as gambling and alcohol drive many people into chaos.
- Decisions on the use of our time for purposeless or selfish activities (including excessive work) can build resentment in our spouses and children. Marriage problems and children's inappropriate conduct erupt out of neglect and misplaced priorities.
- Decisions to engage in unhealthy lifestyles—drugs, alcohol, pornography—ultimately prove destructive. These decisions, even in youth, can produce profound effects for a lifetime.

These poor personal choices reflect what the Bible calls, "the lust of the flesh and the lust of the eyes and the boastful pride of life" (1 John 2:16, NASB).

Other-Induced External Chaos

Sometimes we have little choice or influence in disturbing events that accumulate to push us over the edge into chaos.

- Our children divorce.
- Our children return home broken in spirit and health.
- Our parents experience ill health or death.

✖ We lose our jobs.

✖ We feel pressure at work.

✖ Our health fails.

✖ We are beset by accidents.

These external events, along with the general developments in our rapidly changing world, can drive even the most gifted or stable person to a deep sense of chaos—and discouragement.

Internal Chaos

The Bible is clear in its teaching that the source of most of our problems resides within us—in our minds and hearts. The full list is lengthy, but consider:

✖ Pride that expresses itself in the way we relate to people, accept correction, or blame our failures on others

✖ An inner drivenness to accomplish, accumulate, or achieve at the expense of all else

✖ A refusal to allow God to be a part of our lives—even when we claim to be followers of Christ

✖ Fear of the future and fear of failure

✖ Anxiety that robs us of the joy of living

✖ Resentment toward others who seem to have what we want

✖ Jealousy of the success of others

I believe these are largely spiritual issues that must be addressed with spiritual solutions.

The point of this discussion is to show the multifaceted sources of our chaos. Some have existed as long as man has lived. Others are the result of our times and the culture of speed and technology. We live in a day when all these technological and cultural changes interact with each other in unpredictable ways—which taken together, we call chaos.

A LONGING FOR SIMPLICITY

One of the magazines that has appeared on our coffee table in the past few years is *Reminiscence*. It features pictures and stories of times long past. Simpler times. Less-pressured times. No phone, no e-mail, no DayTimers or Franklin Planners or Palm Pilots, little travel, and families at home for dinner every evening. I wonder if Mary is giving me a message!

In every part of our country, we find antique and gift shops filled with memorabilia. Some antiques are truly valuable. Most simply remind us of a past era that we imagine was more peaceful and far less stressful.

Yet as we examine those times past, we discover women trapped in their kitchens, working all day to prepare meals on a wood or coal stove. Laundry was done by hand, laboriously, consuming hours per week. There was little leisure, no escape. Daily necessities were scraped together with great effort. Life was harsh and short. Before 1920, few families escaped the loss of one or more children to devastating illnesses. Life was hard. Making a living was labor-intensive.

Yet the cycle of life was simpler. Extended families often lived together or near each other. Grandparents and grandchildren were physically close. Options were limited—as were opportunities. The community deeply influenced morality and conduct. On the other hand, relationships and relational conflicts were little different from today's. These small towns and communities were not havens of peace and tranquility.

What is different today is the speed and pace of life, the demands on families to give their children all the activity options (sports, music lessons, and so on), the prevalent materialism (people acquiring nice homes and cars much earlier than their parents had), the greater percentage of both spouses being employed, and the debt that so many incur.

After many years at this pace, we just wear out. We begin to look for ways to cut back and eliminate activities—usually with little success. We read wonderful books on simplifying life, getting a cabin at the lake or mountains (then spending incredible hours and resources fixing them up!), taking longer vacations, and working on an early retirement.

As much as we long for this simplicity to get us out of the chaos and complexity, it still seems to elude us. Thomas Kelly gives us an eloquent explanation:

> Let me first suggest that we are giving a false explanation of the complexity of our lives. We blame it upon the complex environment ... (but) the complexity of our program cannot be blamed upon the complexity of our environment, as much as we would like to think so. Nor will simplification of life follow simplification of environment.
>
> I would suggest that the true explanation of the complexity of our program is an inner one, not an outer one. The outer distractions of our interests reflect an inner lack of integration of our own lives. We are trying to be several selves at once, without all our selves being organized by a single, mastering life within us ...
>
> And we are unhappy, uneasy, strained, oppressed and fearful we shall be shallow. For over the margins of life comes a whisper, a faint call, a premonition of richer living which we know we are passing by ... we have hints that there is a way of life vastly richer and deeper than all this hurried existence, a life of unhurried serenity and peace and power.
>
> We have seen such lives, integrated, unworried by the tangles of close decision, unhurried, cheery, fresh, positive. These are not people of dallying idleness nor obviously mooning meditation; they are busy, carrying their full load as well as we are, but without any chafing of the shoulders with the burden, with quiet joy and springing step ... Life is meant to be lived from a center, a defined center.[1]

Kelly's analysis that the real problem lies within us rings true in the reality of my personal life experience. Activities, pressure to perform, schedules, and demands of people are a reality. The nagging question that we must address is, "What has brought so many complex pressures into our lives?" How much comes from our inner drivenness and our prior decisions that make the current schedule inevitable? Our work and personal commitments tend to fill up all available time—and energy. When we are already pushed to the limit, we have no room for the unexpected incursion of family issues, illness, and events, which push us into overload.

When this happens, what most often gets pushed aside are family and God. Not that we no longer engage in family and religious activities, but rather that they become mere obligations and pressures. They no longer give joy—to them or to us. Our life becomes one of compulsion, not choice.

When I think of simplicity, I cannot help but think of ordinary people who do not have a wide range of choices in life. They work at jobs that give little freedom. They have limited incomes to meet the demands of family, buying a home, educating children, and possessing only a minimum of "extras." Often both spouses work. As I mentioned earlier, so many single mothers and fathers face incredible pressures just to keep life together, without much opportunity to think of simplifying life, as much as they would like to do so. Only a small percentage of people enjoy the luxury of cutting back on their work schedule, taking extended time away, or building a retreat in the mountains or on a lake. If this is true for the majority of Americans, it is so much more the case for those in less-affluent countries.

It is important to recognize that we have only limited control over our environment and circumstances. We must look for solutions in those areas we can control or influence. The primary battle for simplicity lies within. There are several lessons regarding this principle in the Bible.

When Jesus sent the twelve disciples village-to-village, He instructed them, "Don't think you need a lot of extra equipment for this. *You* are the equipment. No special appeals for funds. Keep it simple" (Mark 6:8, MSG). Jesus lived simply. He wanted His disciples to function simply—to learn that they were the message and that their needs would be supplied. The teaching here is certainly one of simplicity, but even more, it is about the concept of taking your marching orders from Jesus. Later Jesus instructed them to take food, clothing, and protection. Each person and each circumstance needs specific direction from God. There are few generalities.

Simplicity is closely connected to contentment. In 1 Timothy 6:6, Paul taught, "But godliness with contentment is great gain." I like the way Eugene Peterson expresses it in *The Message:* "A devout life does bring wealth, but it's the rich simplicity of being yourself before God." There is deep satisfaction in a simple life of faith. The more we are content with the circumstances in which God has placed us, the more freedom we find to make good decisions for our lives. *An inner sense of contentment gives us freedom.*

We can reduce much of life to a decision of whether or not we will focus on our primary devotion to God. As the apostle Paul wrote, "But I am afraid, lest as the serpent deceived Eve by his craftiness, your minds should be led astray from the simplicity and purity of devotion to Christ" (2 Corinthians 11:3, NASB). The context of this statement was Paul's concern that fhe believers in Corinth might leave the purity of the gospel he had presented. It is easy to look for life solutions in places other than the ultimate source—God. Keep your faith in God simple and pure.

CONFRONTING THE EXTREMES

Two extreme views of dealing with chaos and complexity can lead us into difficulty. One obvious response is to accommodate and embrace all the external changes and developments in full. This approach assumes that technological and scientific developments will inevitably engulf our lives and families; consequently, we should learn to adjust our lives to them, regardless of the stresses and pressures they engender. The problem with this approach is a lack of discrimination, simply adding to an already hectic lifestyle. We give in to the pressures of the moment, neglecting to pare down our pace to something that is manageable and even refreshing.

The opposite extreme is to attempt to escape from any impact of the society around us. This would be reflected, as discussed earlier in the chapter, as a drive for simplicity. To this end people quit their jobs, move to rural areas, raise their own food, and attempt to live a life apart from the influence of modern society. This may seem idyllic, but in my view, it neglects the biblical injunction to live among the people of our time. To escape just to save ourselves or our families does not respond to the incredible need of sharing the good news of Jesus Christ with those about us, helping them learn to live in the midst of this chaotic society. It is also a solution that only a very few people can attain. It does not fit the vast majority of Americans, whose options are limited and whose lives are circumscribed with obligations that cannot be easily escaped.

Kevin soon sold his yacht. He began to deepen his commitment to Christ. He began to savor life in a way that he never had before. Did all the problems go away? Not at all. The battle with cancer continued. His business survived, but not without hard work and struggle. But he was a different man, far more content to let God control his life and circumstances. His chaos did not disappear, but he and his wife learned how to work through it.

As we wrestle with chaos and complexity and their counterpoint, simplicity, Phil Mason makes an excellent observation:

Time Waits for No One

When we are small time seems endless—an hour can seem like an age, but as we grow older there doesn't seem enough hours in the day to do all we want to do, and time seems to fly past. Years ago when most people had to work longer hours they usually had time to visit family and friends, to pause in the street for a chat, and even to stand and stare. Maybe with all our modern inventions like the car, television, and telephone, we have lost something, for it seems that many people no longer have time for the little things that make life worthwhile.

CHAPTER 4

NO MAGIC FORMULA

In the movie *Before and After*, the narrator, a young girl, says, "Your whole world can change in a second and you never even know when it's coming. Before, you think you know what kind of a world this is, and after, everything is different for you. Not bad, maybe, not always, but different, forever. I didn't used to know that, till the day it happened to my family. I didn't even know there could be such a thing as after. I didn't know that for us, before was already over."

This young girl is reflecting on the day her teenage brother is accused of murder. The ensuing turmoil threatens to destroy her family. Life never returned to normal for them. The "after" plunged her family into a morass of lies, distrust, intrigue, and despair.

Is there a "before and after" in your life? A point where change, for better or worse, was inevitable?

Reality is harsh. The idyllic life evades us. In its place, real life emerges in ways we never expected. Some better, some worse. Most often that reality disturbs and upsets us. Our marriage, our jobs, our health, or our families take on a life of their own—out of control. The one thing we want is control, and it is the one thing we do not have. We want to determine our destiny. We desperately try. We find that we cannot. We search for that *magic formula* that will miraculously transform our reality into our fantasies.

Life does not work that way. Are there miracles? Certainly. The unexpected and beautiful does surprise us, but often not in ways we anticipated. Each day is full of surprises of beauty and of harsh reality.

Stories of beauty and pleasure are enjoyable to remember. Do you remember when you first met your future husband or wife? I certainly do. Mary had transferred to the University of Washington in her sophomore year after her family moved from Minnesota to Washington. She called a church asking for directions to get there by city bus. They told her that was difficult. And they gave her my name to call about a ride.

She called on a Saturday evening. Saturday night is a rather noisy and fun time at most college residences. When she called, another student yelled down the hall to me. "Who is it?" I called back.

"It's a girl," he said.

You can imagine the banter that ensued as I came to the phone. When I took the phone, Mary said (she denies this!), "What's the matter? Are you afraid of women?"

I went the next day to pick her up. I saw this lovely woman with flaming red hair come down the winding stairway in the classic women's residence. She recalls seeing me. "There he was, in a blue blazer jacket and lime-green checked pants!"

That encounter changed our lives forever.

I enjoy and trust the way the Bible paints the reality of people's lives. It shows people making great mistakes and living with the consequences. It shows heroes with feet of clay. It reveals the good, the bad, and the ugly. Yet God used these people, imperfect as they were. If I were to write Old Testament history, I would paint a much more attractive picture of Abraham, Moses, Samson, David, and Solomon. Yet it wouldn't be real. The Bible tells it like it is. It is not a cover up. That is what lifts it above humanly comprised history to a divine record. It does not pull punches or excuse sin. It does not give tightly woven logic to define its characters' motives. Rather, it presents a picture of man at his worst and best— often the same man.

My children, after being caught in some mistake or wrongdoing, would tell me, "But, Dad, nobody's perfect." They were right. Nobody is perfect. No leader, no boss, no father, no mother, no pastor, no businessperson. All people have chinks in their armor, even when they attempt to hide them. I certainly do, though I do *my* best to hide them. Who wants to be that vulnerable? Eventually, the closer one gets to people, the more one sees their weaknesses.

That is what Paul meant in 2 Corinthians 4:7, "But we have this treasure in jars of clay, to show that the surpassing power belongs to God and not to us" (ESV).

Jars of clay.

Cracked pots.

A fitting description of our humanity.

The Living Bible expresses it well, "But this precious treasure—this light and power that now shine within us—is held in a perishable container, that is, in our weak bodies. Everyone can see that the glorious power within must be from God and is not our own."

The older we get the more we sense our own humanity and frailty, and even our faults. We tolerate them in ourselves. But we find it difficult to tolerate them in others. Yet that is what God wants us to do. He wants us to see our own humanity and then extend grace to others, knowing that we desperately need grace ourselves. This discovery of our humanity with all its failings, coupled with the all-encompassing chaos that inevitably surrounds and impacts us, can lead to much despair and discouragement. Or the discovery can lead to a gratifying opportunity for God to work significant changes in our lives.

Many people reach a point of sensory overload. This produces a helplessness they cannot escape. They cannot focus on anything.

Women may find themselves faced with a less-than-ideal marriage, demanding children, financial pressures, wondering why they did not pursue a career, worried that they cannot support themselves if their marriage fails—and chaos becomes their reality. Men similarly may worry about their jobs, their futures, their battles with lust, their inadequacies as fathers, financial pressure, and a nagging feeling that life has passed them by.

We experience personal chaos, economic chaos, technological chaos, political chaos, social chaos. The combination proves deadly. Psychiatric hospitals, counseling centers, and pastors' offices are filled as people lose hope and can no longer cope. Psychological theories—even the Christian ones—give only temporary relief. We pray and see no answers. We work harder and become more discouraged and desperate.

Many give up. Some absent themselves from fellowship with other believers. Others discard the spiritual habits that once encouraged them. And others just learn to tolerate a shallow life, believing that they cannot escape the deadening chaos that has dulled their inner lives. They live with the pain of lack of hope. Still others find themselves turning away from God.

We read books—even write them—to attempt to find some escape from the dilemmas. But there is no escape.

Carol is a beautiful young woman who had great hopes for her life. She married, only to find her husband was an alcoholic and physically abusive. She finally divorced him to protect her two children. She was holding down a respectable managerial job—low paying, but adequate. She was unjustly fired from the position. She then upgraded her education, finally securing a much better job. Yet she still suffers from anxiety and depression. Her parents give her no help. Every time she begins a romantic relationship, she finds it is a dead end. She feels she is "hanging on by her fingernails," desperately hoping life will get better. But, reluctantly, she sees no way out.

I remember Thomas. He was a promising athlete on a scholarship to an excellent university that did not give athletes any academic excuses. He flunked out in his final year. He married quickly, so he had to support a family. It took him years to finish his education. His jobs were never fully satisfying. He has an excellent walk with God, but puzzles over his lack of ability to "get it together." Very little ever seems to work out well for him.

Carol and Thomas experience the dilemma of so many in a chaotic life, with no sign that it will end.

> *Therefore we do not lose heart. Though outwardly we are wasting away, yet inwardly we are being renewed day by day. For our light and momentary troubles are achieving for us an eternal glory that far outweighs them all. So we fix our eyes not on what is seen, but on what is unseen. For what is seen is temporary, but what is unseen is eternal.*
> 2 Corinthians 4:16-18

LIFE RUNNING DOWN AND BEING REBUILT

Life is wasting away in the outward and bodily sense. From the moment we are born, we begin to die. No one lasts forever. In our youth this fact has almost no relevance. We think we are indestructible. Even with brief glimpses into illness and death, it does not fully sink in.

At some inevitable time, we experience a break in our health. Suddenly, our mortality confronts us and we begin to understand. Paul speaks of being inwardly renewed day by day. What does that mean? Is it some magic transformation? No, it is the gradual, almost imperceptible, building of an inner life with God that keeps us living in hope.

Verse 17 speaks of troubles that are temporary—"light and momentary." When we are experiencing these troubles, they seem anything but light or momentary. They seem interminable and heavy. We understand that something deep is taking place within us. We cannot control or create it. We glimpse a future that is bright, but the fact of our problems impacts our lives in the present.

Our lives consist of hopes and dreams for the future laced with experiences from the past. Past experience takes on more authority the longer we live. Then our hopes and dreams are either poisoned or energized by the past. That is reality. In that process we can become cynical or hopeless. This leads to a consuming staleness.

Albert Schweitzer once wrote, "The tragedy of life is not that one dies, but that one dies while he still lives."

Anne Frank, the Jewish school girl whose diary from her World War II captivity penetrated the hurts of so many, spoke of a vision of the future: "I see the world gradually being turned into a wilderness. I hear the ever approaching thunder, which will destroy us too. I can feel the sufferings of millions and yet, if I look up into the heavens, I think it will all come right, that this cruelty too will end, and that peace and tranquility will return again."[1]

Hope comes from our faith. Hope keeps us going. Hope energizes.

One of the hard facts of life is that we are dying from the moment we are born. Certainly, after reaching adulthood we see the unmistakable signs of life running down. We are faced with our own mortality. Paul beats this drum again in 2 Corinthians 4:16: "That is why we never give up. Though our bodies are dying, our inner strength in the Lord is growing every day" (TLB).

Too often we are tempted to give up. When life becomes

chaotic and difficult, we long to give up or at least withdraw. Paul contemplates that.

> These troubles and sufferings of ours are, after all, quite small and won't last very long. Yet this short time of distress will result in God's richest blessing upon us forever and ever! So we do not look at what we can see right now, the troubles all around us, but we look forward to the joys in heaven which we have not yet seen. The troubles will soon be over, but the joys to come will last forever. (2 Corinthians 4:17-18, TLB)

If we fail to gain our strength and focus in Christ, we face a new formula:

Humanity + Chaos = Despair and Discouragement

Even as we long for a release from chaos, we slip deeper into discouragements. We understand in our minds that eternal life in heaven will bring peace and pleasure, but we don't want to wait until heaven. We want the joy now. Right now!

When I was a Ph.D. student at Purdue University, I noticed that the sidewalks on campus crisscrossed the beautiful lawns at seemingly random and crazy angles. I soon found out why. Some wise groundskeepers simply saw where the students wore down the grass, and they proceeded to lay the sidewalks over those trails! The groundskeeper responded with a plan to match reality!

We all want shortcuts—to happiness, to success, to health, to everything of value. Most shortcuts do not work. They lead to disappointment and disaster, disillusionment and failure. For the things in life that count the most, there are no lottery winners, no instant riches, no immediate happiness.

Instead there are myths, precepts, and beliefs that deceive us. There are pipe dreams—the hallucinations of a hashish pipe smoker that blur and vanish in the light of reality. There are fairy tales—stories that sound great but lead to sadness and cynicism when we find they do not work.

God is not under any obligation to prosper us materially. He does promise to meet our needs in every circumstance of life, which can be to help us survive in adverse conditions and even to be joyful in difficult times.

MYTHS

Myth 1: God Must Prosper Us Materially.

This myth is pervasive in some Christian teachings. In the Old Testament, God does promise prosperity to Israel for their continued obedience: "But remember the LORD your God, for it is he who gives you the ability to produce wealth, and so confirms his covenant, which he swore to your forefathers, as it is today" (Deuteronomy 8:18). The Psalms often speak of God's blessing on a holy life. Yet we fail to realize the context of those words and the associated curses for disobedience. The focus of these Scriptures is primarily related to the nation of Israel, regarding the consequences of obedience and disobedience.

One brief glance at the world and its many true believers should dispel this notion. They suffer poverty, persecution, and hunger. They are mistreated and murdered. It has been said that there were more martyrs in the twentieth century than the combined total in the previous nineteen centuries.

In Deuteronomy 5:32-33, God told Israel before entering the Promised Land that *if* they obeyed all the commands He had given them they would "live and prosper and prolong your days in the land that you will possess." This was written to Israel as a nation, not to individuals. This is clear in that there were many individuals who continued to follow God, such as the godly prophets, but the nation was still exiled because of their disobedience. It was the same context in the much-quoted Joshua 1:8: "Then you will be prosperous and successful." A similar promise was often given to the kings and leaders in the Old Testament.

One of Job's friends and tormentors told him, "Submit to God and be at peace with him; in this way prosperity will come to you" (Job 22:21; see also 36:11). He said this because he had concluded that Job had sinned, which was not why trouble had come upon Job. Job later became prosperous, but not for the reasons his friends had said.

In the Psalms, the word *prosperity* comes from the Hebrew word for "peace," *shalom,* or the Hebrew word for "benefit or welfare." God will give peace for obedience and will care for our welfare. But He does not promise material wealth or financial prosperity.

There is no guarantee of material prosperity in this life. God does promise to meet our "needs." In our Western affluence we easily assume that we deserve material success and prosperity. We live at a rare time in history where believers in Christ are honored and respected. Wealth is not unusual for some followers of Jesus. Yet riches are not the norm, even in the West. As we survey the world, we see persecution, martyrdom, and deep poverty among believers. They are no less godly than anyone in the affluent West.

As I travel around the world, I meet men and women who are godly and highly gifted. Yet because of their faith, their tribal circumstances, or their societal position, they will never be economically prosperous. One such man, an engineer, drives a taxi, hardly making enough to support his family. Another man lives in constant fear of arrest as he leads and encourages other believers. He keeps a bag packed in his closet with clothes and medications to take with him to jail when he is arrested.

When God permits us to have comfort, wealth, and success, we should be thankful, but not proud. God is not obligated to provide in abundance. One of the doctrinal errors Paul described to his friend and protégé Timothy was about "men of corrupt mind . . . who think that godliness is a means to financial gain" (1 Timothy 6:5). The truth is that

> Godliness with contentment is great gain. For we brought nothing into the world, and we can take nothing out of it. But if we have food and clothing, we will be content with that. People who want to get rich fall into temptation and a trap and into many foolish and harmful desires that plunge men into ruin and destruction. For the love of money is a root of all kinds of evil. Some people, eager for money, have wandered from the faith and pierced themselves with many griefs. (1 Timothy 6:6-10)

It is quite clear that there is no formal connection between godliness and wealth. Paul recognizes that there were wealthy believers, many of whom supported both Jesus and Paul. To them he said,

> Command those who are rich in this present world not to be arrogant nor to put their hope in wealth, which is so uncertain, but to put their hope in God, who richly provides us with everything for our enjoyment. Command them to do good, to be rich in good deeds, and to be generous and willing to share. In this way they will lay up treasure for themselves as a firm foundation for the coming age, so that they may take hold of the life that is truly life. (1 Timothy 6:17-19)

Contentment is the key. The responsibility of wealth must lead to generosity, not arrogance.

No amount of money or prestige will buy our way out of chaos. Chaos permeates the palaces of kings and the lives of the wealthy and powerful. This is clear as we observe the accounts in the media of people in positions of wealth and power. Rarely does one see happiness and peace.

Fame and success often ruin people rather than help them. Marilyn Monroe became an international sex symbol. After three marriages and her self-imposed demand to be a respected actress, not just a sex symbol, she committed suicide at the age of thirty-six.

Ernest Hemingway won the 1954 Nobel Prize in Literature. He was both prolific in his writing and famous. After three marriages and great public success, he killed himself with a shotgun.

Money, success, and fame do not satisfy.

Myth 2: There Are Guaranteed Steps to Escape the Effects of Chaos.

As chaos envelops and invades our lives, we search for answers, an escape, or a way out. We read books, attend seminars, and listen to motivational talks on "getting

Christian millionaire, John D. Rockefeller, said, "I have made many millions, but they have brought me no happiness. I would barter them all for the days I sat on an office stool in Cleveland and counted myself rich on three dollars a week." (Broken in health, he employed an armed guard.)

W. H. Vanderbilt said, "The care of 200 million dollars is too great a load for any brain or back to bear. It is enough to kill anyone. There is no pleasure in it."

John Jacob Astor left five million, but had been martyr to dyspepsia and melancholy. He said, "I am the most miserable man on earth."[2]

67

control of your life." We search for some means of eluding the complexity and intensity as we are impacted by chaos.

Chaos fills our surroundings like the air we breathe. Air exists and we must breathe it to live. Chaos too is a reality of life. Trying to escape chaos is like arguing with the wind or the ocean. Prevailing is impossible. No one escapes the effects of chaos. Run as we will from technology, economic reality, and sweeping changes in the workplace, we will inevitably be affected.

There are no guaranteed steps to follow—even in this book!

Certainly, principles exist that help us walk through these times. But just as we are unique individuals, just as our circumstances, personalities, and families are different, so we need personalized solutions. One person's "way out" is not another's. God counsels each individual by saying, "This is the way; walk in it" (Isaiah 30:21). God provides a circumscribed path for every individual.

Engineers and artists approach life differently. The engineer wants plans and procedures to achieve a predicted outcome. The artist does not "paint by the numbers" but responds to a vision of what can be, and paints or sculpts an image unique in history.

We need to see our lives as the work of an artist—and to respond creatively each day.

Myth 3: It Will Get Better with Time, so Just Wait.

Chaos generally does not get better with time. History witnesses to that fact. The delay of the United States to enter into World War II may be one of recent history's lessons of the dangers of waiting.

The saying "Don't just sit there, do something" may fit well here. Inattention, inactivity, or ignorance does not solve our problems. While it is true that patience is a virtue, patience does not change reality. There are seasons and times of extensive chaos in which patience must be exercised to see wise strategies for coping work. But doing nothing is most often a poor strategy.

A weather bulletin for tornadoes or tropical storms requires action. A collapsing economy requires a response. An exploding marriage or family catastrophe needs healing action. After we have done all that we can wisely do, then waiting is proper—and needed. A head-in-the-sand approach to both our inner and our outer chaos will certainly lead to disaster.

Myth 4: If I Live a More Spiritual Life, I Will Not Be Impacted by the Chaos Around Me.

We certainly should live a more spiritual life. But all our spirituality will not keep the external chaos from affecting us and our families—our jobs and communities. As we experience the effects of chaos both inwardly and outwardly, we should seek a deeper life with God. That will help us endure chaos—even grow stronger through it. But we still will be influenced and impacted. We may need to change jobs or careers. We may need to think differently about our lifestyle, our family, our desires, or our pace of life. The most spiritual people in the Bible were caught up in the trauma and chaos of their time.

Who could imagine more chaotic and stressful times than Moses encountered in the incredible slavery of his people in Egypt? The last forty years of his life embodied a level of chaos that most of us will never experience.

The great persecutions under Nero in the first century affected everyone. People were driven out of their homes and countries. They were persecuted. They were destroyed economically.

Nero was a cruel, narcissistic ruler who left a trail of turmoil and suffering throughout the Roman Empire. Thousands of citizens were caught up and crushed in the wake of his destructive leadership.

The corruption of kings and governments has, through the centuries, affected both believers and nonbelievers alike. Injustice is not a respecter of persons.

A spiritual focus will provide a basis, a foundation, for walking calmly through personal and national chaos, but it will not prevent it.

Myth 5: If I Radically Simplify My Life, I Will Solve My Chaos Problem.

As I mentioned earlier, a new genre of publications has emerged on the market—and on the coffee table! They are magazines that take us down memory lane (depending on your age!). They depict scenes of small towns, Grandma's farm kitchen, roasting turkeys, hand-prepared foods, families gathered around old radios. They appeal to the desire to turn back the clock, to return to simpler times.

I have memories of a simple life in a small farm community of Iowa where I spent the first nine years of my life. There is only one problem. Life was not simple. It was hard and demanding, even though my childhood memories are idyllic and pleasant.

But it was far from easy for the adults of those previous generations. Life was relationally complex. Communities were ingrown with prejudice and conflicts. Work required hard physical labor. Homes and food preparation demanded constant, all-day attention. Leisure activities were scarce. Health care was limited. Life spans were short. Admittedly, the pace of life was slower. Change did not occur as quickly as it does today.

The question is, Can we return to those days? The answer is, "No." Can we simplify our lives? Yes, to some degree. Will that simplifying solve our chaos problems? No. Chaos still exists. We might reduce the impact slightly, but our children, friends, and relatives will continue to live in the world we try to simplify.

By *simplify,* many think "escape." I applaud the idea of simplifying life—wanting to do it myself. But I do not applaud the idea of escaping from the mainstream of society. Simplifying our lifestyles can be a luxury few can afford—a second home, a cabin by a lake, a job with fewer demands. Often, the more we possess, the more we invite chaos into our lives as we struggle to maintain our belongings. We still live with the obligations of children in school, debts to pay, and community responsibilities.

The majority of the people in the United States and other countries do not have the means to change their circumstances to escape.

Simplifying life is one of the strategies for coping, but not in the way we imagine and not in the idyllic pictures painted in the magazines on the coffee table.

PIPE DREAMS

Pipe Dream 1: There Is an Idyllic Perfect Future and I Can Create It.

As we are growing up, we dream of the future—what it will be like, what marriage will be, what our career will be. The dreams are filled with pleasures and success, not with the reality of life as we come to know it later. These dreams are not harmful. Often they motivate us to work hard. But only God can create a future. We can be deceived by the idea that we are totally in control of our future. It is our responsibility to prepare but it is God's to fulfill and create. What we want is God's future for us, with all its complications and blessings.

Pipe Dream 2: There Is One Perfect Way to Live.

We are not clones. We are individuals with separate gifts, needs, desires, and callings. Each person is answerable to

God for his or her lifestyle, use of time and energy, focus, job choices, and societal involvements. While basic principles and values should direct us all, the outworking of those principles and values can look quite different.

I have attended conferences and read books that urged me to change to a certain pattern of living. I felt guilt that my present life did not quite conform to their ideal. Then I wrestled with whether I was wrong, living sinfully, selfishly, or foolishly.

I soon learned that I need to pick and choose from these diverse inputs to adopt what fit me and my family. As a leader and speaker, I too cross the line when urging people to conform to my way of thinking or teaching. That is the nature of human leadership—to influence the lives and actions of others. But the humility of godly leadership is to recognize that each person is unique, and no one should follow without carefully considering the truth and personal appropriateness of the leader's message.

We should all be like the Berean people in Acts 17:11: "Now the Bereans were of more noble character than the Thessalonians, for they received the message with great eagerness and examined the Scriptures every day to see if what Paul said was true." Each of us is responsible to live well by a set of standards only we can determine—from the Bible, from God directly, and from the counsel of godly friends. What I say in this book must be considered only if it makes sense under scrutiny and prayerful consideration. I see my role as stirring you to think carefully and biblically, and to give you ideas, not directions, of how to proceed.

Pipe Dream 3: The Latter Part of My Life Will Be Easier and Simpler.

How I wish this were true. The empty nest, the freedom of the last half of life, retirement, or perhaps the peak of a career—each appeals to our desire for some release from the pressures of the daily grind.

For those of you already at that stage of life, you have already given your answer. Bunk! Life does not get simpler or easier. Grandchildren, family, health concerns, declining job opportunities, instability in the employment market, and financial pressure all add to the chaos of pressured lives as we grow older.

There are changes for the good. Hopefully, we have become wiser, more realistic, and less materialistic, which gives promise and hope for a more contented life—but not an easier one. Let's not live in dread of the future, but also let's not believe pipe dreams are true.

Pipe Dream 4: There Will Be Increasing Ease as Technology Lifts My Load.

At the turn of the year 2000, the *Wall Street Journal* published a fascinating list of predictions of what life would be like at the start of the twenty-first century.[3]

In 1950, *Popular Mechanics* predicted, "The housewife of 2000 can do her daily cleaning with a garden hose. Why not? Thanks to plastics, everything is waterproof. True for washing down dairy barns!"[4]

In 1893, Mary Lease, a reformer, at the Chicago World's Fair said, "Three hours will constitute a long day's work by the end of the next century. And this work will liberally furnish infinitely more of the benefits of civilization and the comforts of life than 16 hours slavish toil will today."[5]

Nothing could have been more wrong. We live with the reality of longer hours, two-job families, and increasing pressure with less leisure.

Technology certainly is a friend in many areas of life. But as we saw earlier, technology is largely responsible for the increasing chaos of our age. That is not likely to change in the next few decades.

FAIRY TALES

Fairy tales are characterized by difficult problems overcome by heroes of great prowess with the players living happily ever after. Our lives are imbued with certain fairy tales from our youth onward. Here are a few:

Fairy Tale 1: We Will Live Happily Ever After.

In this life we know this is not true. The idyllic marriage turns into a living hell. The perfect job brings stress and disillusionment with leaders and owners.

There is no guarantee of a happy life. Happiness takes work, compromises, and adjustment of expectations. Life is not simple; neither is it continually happy.

On reflection, almost everyone would say that one of their greatest desires is for a happy life. That happiness is variously defined but certainly includes personal relationships as a major element. It would also include inner peace.

Happiness is extremely elusive. It is difficult to define, difficult to find. It is subjective—dependent on desires and expectations. As we grow and mature, our definition of true happiness changes.

Fairy Tale 2: All Technological and Material Advances Are Bad.

Do you remember when bar codes on food and retail goods were introduced? Religious books and radio programs warned of a satanic plot, the "mark of the beast." Obviously it was not. It advanced the management of goods, sales, and checkouts, and it opened many jobs to less-skilled labor. Today bar codes are on almost every item we touch—from computers to clothes to cars.

With the invention of the airplane some said, "If God had intended man to fly, He would have given us wings." Almost every technological advance has had its religious and secular detractors.

But in the main, technological advances serve humanity. Discoveries lighten our daily workload, advance health care, open doors of discovery, create new careers and jobs, and connect the world.

In the spiritual realm we can now send missionaries to remote parts of the world, keep in touch daily by e-mail, and fly them home cheaply for emergencies or children's education.

In the early days of missions, missionaries packed their goods in coffins and often died in the first year on the field. Today, through communication and media, the Bible and spiritual truth are increasingly accessible throughout the world.

Scientific advances are our friends, not our enemies. They require change. They challenge our way of living and doing business. Let's welcome the invasion of advances into our lives.

Fairy Tale 3: All Technological and Material Advances Are Good.

Nuclear energy ended World War II, thrusting us into a future of fear and danger unprecedented in history. With the welcome advances of nuclear medicine, nuclear power, and related products come the burdens of guarding the misuse of such incredible power. It is not all good.

In many fields, that which is invented for good creates danger and havoc in the wrong hands. With the internal combustion engine came a new wave of pollution replacing the pollution created daily by horse dung, which was a bane to every city in earlier centuries.

With the pervasive influence and availability of television and video products came a new way to educate and influence the public. It also introduced a new proliferation in the billion-dollar business of pornography and a teaching of values abhorrent to so many of us.

The new advances in biogenetics raise the specter of genetic manipulation and of cloning test-tube humans. These advances also give promise of cures for devastating diseases.

No, these advances are not all good, but they are relentless. We cannot easily keep "progress" from happening. Nor, if one gives careful thought, should we fight it. As in every great discovery of the past, good people should fight to harness and control these advances for the good of mankind. Spiritually minded believers must be involved. We must never pull into our shells, hide in the mountains, and say, "I can't control the future, but I can protect my children and our way of life." A bit of history quickly reveals the folly of such an approach.

Fairy Tale 4: One Marriage, One Career, One Family Are the Norm for an Idyllic Life.

I can see the hair raising on the backs of the necks of some of you reading this! Isn't this our ideal? Certainly, one marriage and one family is our ideal. The reality is that almost half of you reading this book have been divorced. Far more than that have parents, siblings, or close friends who are divorced. We cannot escape this reality. A life unaffected by family turmoil, divorce, and blended families is a fairy tale. It will not happen.

That does not mean that we should give up fighting for the ideal, but we must not ostracize those whose lives have been deeply wounded by the breakup of families. Their reality can be impacted by God's love and power and can be a path to joy in spite of their personal history. This is no soft-on-divorce appeal. Rather, it is a plea for deep caring and understanding of millions whose lives desperately need the infusion of God's forgiving love and new beginnings available in Jesus.

I know of no greater chaos than that caused by the breakup of marriages and families. We must walk through this chaos with neighbors, relatives, and friends. As I view Mary's and my forty-plus years of marriage, I realize how blessed we are. Yet we both look back on times of stress and conflict that could easily have led to disaster. In a prevailing culture that devalues marriage commitment, we realize that most do not enter marriage with the lifelong understanding we did. I am the son of divorce, so I know firsthand the impact of the splitting of families.

One career? As I stated in chapter 2, this idea disappeared over twenty-five years ago. One of the greatest dilemmas of young people today is that career fields change so quickly that they find it difficult to even settle on a course of study. Most over forty-five have seen their original career change drastically or even disappear.

Fairy Tale 5: The "Good Guys" Always Win.

We want to believe that the good will always triumph. Again, history does not bear this out. Even our personal experiences in business, the workplace, corporations, and life show this to be a fairy tale. Good people often get crunched. Many do succeed and win, but just as many suffer injustice and wrong.

In the less-developed world, where corruption prevails, it is rare for good to triumph. Most often, evil triumphs. That was the plaintive cry and question of Solomon: "In this meaningless life of mine I have seen both of these: a righteous man perishing in his righteousness, and a wicked man living long in his wickedness" (Ecclesiastes 7:15).

The psalmist Asaph saw it too: "This is what the wicked are like—always carefree, they increase in wealth. Surely in vain have I kept my heart pure; in vain have I washed my hands in innocence" (Psalm 73:12-13).

Ancient Job complained, "Why do the wicked live on, growing old and increasing in power?" (Job 21:7).

In the New Testament, Jesus and John the Baptist were killed unjustly.

In this life the good people do not always win. But justice has a long memory. There is an ultimate reckoning. The promise is, "He [God] will judge the world in righteousness; he will govern the peoples with justice" (Psalm 9:8).

In one of the most noted prophecies of Jesus the Messiah, the Bible says, "He will reign on David's throne and over his kingdom, establishing and upholding it with justice and righteousness from that time on and forever" (Isaiah 9:7; see the prophetic fulfillment in Matthew 12:18-21).

Evil people seldom live out their lives in happiness, though they might appear to be prosperous. In this life there is an inner reckoning, even if it does not appear externally.

We see that there is no magic formula. The path through chaos is an individual path. There are many specific paths to get to the same destination. I am not speaking of ways to salvation in Christ, but many paths to successfully walk through life chaos. Now, having shattered some misconceptions, let's chart a principled path through chaos and complexity.

CHAPTER 5

THE PURSUIT OF POWER

Bruce was a man who dreamed of power from his grade-school years. He grew up with a slight speech impediment. The children in his class taunted him, and because he was small in stature, they also isolated him. He resented it and began to dream of revenge. He longed to be strong enough to fight back. He imagined being articulate enough to speak back.

He was intelligent and excelled in his studies. He had average athletic ability. His father had been an outstanding athlete and pushed him continuously to improve. His mother didn't care about athletics but pushed him academically. Bruce's motivation came from neither of them. He simply wanted to be bigger, better, and smarter than the rest—and to win. He wanted power, though that was not the word that he used in those early years.

Near the end of junior high school he went through a growth spurt and began to excel in athletics. Therapy helped him overcome his speech problems. And he was still smart. He received his first taste of real power when he ran for student-body president in high school. He was reasonably popular but ruthlessly began to campaign. He learned how to manipulate people to get them to work for him. And he won! He never gave in to the base desire to be physically abusive to anyone. He was subtle. He learned to humiliate his opponents in other ways.

When he entered university he didn't even consider athletics. He recognized he lacked the talent to compete at that level. He learned other paths to power. He both thought of and used the word *power*. That was what he wanted. Power. Power with many facets.

He took a double major in computer science and business. In his third year of university, he founded a software company with a narrow, specialized product. By the time he graduated, he and his partners owned a successful business.

After graduation he concentrated on the business—one-hundred-hour work weeks, no vacations, driving his growing stable of employees. He became determined to be a millionaire by age thirty. Along the way Bruce fell in love, married, and had two children. His wife, Gail, knew before their marriage about his drive and his ambition. He told her that she and their future family would need to understand his priorities. She agreed, not fully understanding the implications for their marriage and family.

By age thirty, Bruce had achieved far beyond his million. He realized that the power he really wanted was not the power of money, but the power to control people and events. He related well with people but never allowed relationships to become personal. He simply used people—and in his employ, they benefited too. He became a man of power. He was well known. He had all the props and playthings of wealth. He joined the right clubs and attended prestigious social events. But he felt dissatisfied. He sensed the growing tension and distance between himself and Gail. He hardly knew his children. At the end of the day there was no longer a sense of accomplishment.

About four years earlier, Gail had begun to realize that power was not a relationship. She felt used. Although she and Bruce were faithful sexually to one another, their marriage was empty. The qualities that drew her to Bruce—his aggressiveness, his strengths, his ambitions—began to take on new meaning as he demonstrated an irrational lust for power and ruthlessness in business. When Gail tried to express her feelings, he simply referred to their original agreement. Gail became progressively more lonely and dissatisfied in the midst of all the luxury one could want. She and the children lacked for nothing—except a real husband and father.

The handwriting was on the wall. She could see the future and was frightened. She saw a path of frustration and conflict, ending in divorce. They had little time for religion but somehow knew that God, whoever He was, wanted something better for them. Bruce, sensing all of this, knew no solutions. He still wanted power but was powerless to control his own family and marriage—and even his own emotions.

He thought of an affair. He'd often had the opportunity, but rejected the temptation—probably some moral hang-up from his grandparents, he thought. One thing he did know— the power he had sought and achieved did not satisfy him.

Colonel Jack Swenson was walking out of the general's office as I walked into the secretarial area. I asked him the hackneyed question, "How are you doing, Jack?" His reply was not what I expected. "Not so good. I just told the boss that if he had any plans on my competing for promotion to general, he should forget it. I'm out of the hunt!"

When I asked him why, he asked if I had a few minutes to talk. We went to my office and he told me this story: "I have always been an achiever and a pusher. I gave everything my very best. When I was recently promoted to full colonel, they gave me a big promotion party. It was all so positive and upbeat. When we got home, my wife told me all the good things people said about me. 'Greatest boss. Always concerned. When I was in the hospital, he came to see me. He always had time to talk. I've never worked for a more considerate commander.' Then she said, 'Jack, why don't you do that at home? For me and the kids?'" And she packed her bags and left.

Jack was devastated. We talked about God and spiritual issues. I prayed with him and gave him a few words of counsel. He changed his entire lifestyle. He came home at five. He didn't work weekends. He gave his wife space to meet some of her goals, such as finishing a college degree. The process lasted three or four years. But they saved their marriage.

Eventually, he was promoted to general. Jack learned how to use and appreciate real power for his life.

These stories are common. Men and women are swept up in a power chase, only to rarely achieve it—or if they do, their lives are destroyed.

Power is dangerous. Power is elusive. Power is incredibly tempting. Power is a drug that controls. More is always better. From children to teens to young adults to older men and women, we all want to be powerful in some way. The means and definition change, but the desire remains.

You recall from earlier discussions that chaos impacts us deeply because we cannot control it. Chaos represents a lack of power—the inability to control our circumstances. Every human has the inborn drive to want to control people, money, business, children, church, or health. That is the desire for power.

Let's list the various kinds of power:
- Power of wealth
- Power of ownership
- Power of personality
- Power of position
- Power of authority

- Power of knowledge
- Power of relationships
- Power of ability
- Power of character
- Power of spiritual influence
- Power of wisdom

Power as a word by itself has no meaning. Only when connected with some medium or object does power become defined. A medium is all-important to our understanding of power. For instance, when we speak of the "power of God," we immediately imply a full range of all-encompassing power without limits. But when we say the "power of words," we mean a very narrow definition constrained to how powerfully one uses language.

In the accounts above, power is related to wealth, authority, and control of events and people. When men and women seek that kind of power, they are asking for respect and admiration—and occasionally, envy and fear. But that kind of power *never* satisfies for very long. That kind of power may not be evil or wrong, depending on how it is used. That is why we pray for kings and those in authority. They can make an incredible difference in so many people's lives. An evil or good leader, king, or official can set the pattern for a nation, a city, or a company. When such power is selfishly desired and used, then problems erupt—both for the person wielding power and for those subjected to that power.

Almost every kind of power can be used for good or evil. An obvious example is nuclear power. A bomb is incredibly devastating. As a producer of electricity or in a medical intervention, nuclear power is truly beneficial.

I believe everyone wants some kind of power. Henry Kissinger once said, "Power is the ultimate aphrodisiac." But not everyone wants the same kind of power. Let's first examine some of the types of power. Then we will consider the means and motivation for achieving such power.

MAJOR TYPES OF POWER

We have already described the power of wealth and possessions. They are the most known and understood. Where appropriate, I will include some statements from the Bible as it addresses a particular kind of power.

The Power of Authority

Authority comes from various sources. Position is one source. Also, authority is both given and earned. It is given by those who respond to one in authority. It is earned through good leadership. It is not always the one in the position who wields the power. If you depend only on position for authority and power, you will soon lose it. Many achieve authority by personality, knowledge, wisdom, spiritual influence, or ability. Fathers, mothers, friends, coworkers, and leaders hold authority in families, companies, churches, social organizations, and governments.

The Bible is filled with stories and instructions regarding people in authority. Jesus commented,

> "You know that the rulers of the Gentiles lord it over them, and their high officials exercise authority over them. Not so with you. Instead, whoever wants to become great among you must be your servant, and whoever wants to be first must be your slave—just as the Son of Man did not come to be served but to serve, and to give his life a ransom for many." (Matthew 20:25-28)

Jesus said that the kind of authority to be exercised must not be one of lording it over other people or controlling them for one's personal interests. But rather, authority presents an opportunity to serve.

The Power of Knowledge

This is a wonderful kind of authority. When a person is a demonstrated expert in some field, people both know it and listen. Whether in medicine, electronics, building, leadership, family dynamics, or business, such knowledge is unusually persuasive. People of knowledge can be wrong. Yet they do exert power.

I recall the welcoming speech by the dean of faculty at the U.S. Air Force Academy when I joined the faculty: "Remember, you are an expert in only one field. Don't presume that you are an expert in everything." Good advice. But often we see Doctor Somebody, an expert in some field of study, deferred to in areas far beyond his or her knowledge or expertise. Frequently in magazines or on television, a movie star or sports figure expounds on weighty matters, offering political opinions or giving views on which he or she has no experience. This abuse of power can be misleading or even damaging.

I once conducted a seminar on evolution and creation, talking about biology and geology. When it ended I thought, "I'll never do that again." I was so far removed from my expertise in engineering and astronautics that it was ludicrous for me to speak on biology and geology. I had not even studied biology in high school!

A Chinese proverb says, "Know what you know and know what you do not know. That is the mark of a wise man."

The Power of Relationships

Remember the statement, "It is not what you know, but who you know that counts." So true. Most things in this world get done through relationships. I travel in many developing countries, and I see that this is the way of life and business. Is it fair? Not always. It is a fact of life.

At this age and stage of my life, I am blessed with an extensive network of relationships. In almost every difficult situation—finances, medicine, legal issues—I know someone who can help. If they are friends, they want to help. That is power to get things done.

Many people do not have these relationships. For those who do, the opportunity is ripe to help others.

My parents were ordinary, average, hard-working people. In her early sixties, my mother became ill. The doctors could not find the problem and even suggested it was psychosomatic. I finally became frustrated and began tracking a competent diagnostician through friends. When he finally examined my mother, he discovered uterine cancer. My mother soon died at the young age of sixty-two. My parents simply had not known what to do. Their family doctor was their authority.

This illustrates the power of relationships in accomplishing—or not accomplishing—things. But there is more. There is the power of relationships to build us up, to encourage us, to comfort us, and to bring enjoyment to our lives.

The Power of Ability

This is similar to the power of knowledge. Ability is knowledge with gifting applied. We respect people of great ability—craftsmen, actors, speakers, surgeons, artists, leaders, pilots, athletes. Skills with people, with numbers, with words, with mechanical devices—all give people certain power.

I am not skilled in repairing things. I once gave Mary a book for her birthday entitled *Home Repairs Without a Man*. And she uses it! I know my limits in this area. No one ever, ever calls me to fix things (except my grandchildren, who have not quite figured out that I am not Superman).

It is very helpful to know people of skill. When I have computer problems, I call Doug or Bill. When I need financial help, I call Ed or Bob. When I need help finding things around the home, I ask Mary!

Skill opens so many doors. "Do you see a man skillful in his work? He will stand before kings; he will not stand before obscure men" (Proverbs 22:29, ESV).

The Power of Character

Who you are is much more important than what you do. Most of us believe that. Character counts. It undergirds a person's integrity. It gives incredible power. Character leads to trust. What a person of character says is true. They do what they say they will do. Character is the most fundamental element I look for in a leader.

I have seen people of remarkable ability and knowledge whom I would not trust to do anything of importance. They were self-serving and rarely sacrificed for the good of others.

I am pleased to say that in my thirty-seven years in the Air Force (active and reserve), I observed many generals in leadership. I was impressed with their integrity and character. Very few were self-serv-

> *A man who lives right, and is right, has more power in his silence than another has by his words. Character is like bells which ring out sweet music and which, when touched, accidentally even, resound with sweet music.*[1]
> Phillips Brooks

> *Fame is a vapor, popularity an accident, riches take wings. Only one thing endures and that is character.*[2]
> Abraham Lincoln

ing. Those who were, seldom received further promotion. I am proud to have served with them. I learned from them.

Character shows the most in the home. Fathers and mothers who live with spiritual and moral integrity before their children wield great power for the future. It is of no value to achieve in the marketplace, church, or community and yet fail to live with integrity within one's marriage and family. Good

> *Character is the bedrock on which the whole edifice of leadership rests. It is the prime element for which every profession, every corporation, every industry searches in evaluating a member of its organization. With it, the full worth of an individual can be developed. Without it—particularly in the military professions—failure in peace, disaster in war, or at best, mediocrity in both will result.*
>
> General Matthew Ridgway

character does not guarantee that your children will respect you or follow your example completely. But over a lifetime, they will see godly character and honor it.

People of character demonstrate and tell truth. That is power.

The Power of Wisdom

Most of us possess an intuitive appreciation and recognition of wisdom. We know that it is not simply knowledge or authority. Wisdom is knowledge applied. Wisdom is insight regarding the events of history. Wisdom is an understanding of the times and of life events. Wisdom is the ability to sort out truth and value in the noise of the chaos around us.

The wise man of Proverbs shows how wisdom begins: "The fear of the LORD is the beginning of wisdom, and the knowledge of the Holy One is understanding" (Proverbs 9:10). In this context the word *fear* contains both the obvious use of being afraid and the associated idea of recognizing the awesome power and authority of God as the source of all wisdom.

There are wise men and women who are not spiritually minded. They can discern many issues of life. How do they do that? By using the gifts and mind that God has created within them. When they are selfless and compassionate people, they can give wise counsel. When they possess specialized knowledge, they are adept at helping people.

Many times I have gone to people who were not believers for counsel when I know that they are also people of character and unusual ability. They lack insight directly from God, finding it difficult to include a deeply spiritual dimension in their counsel. But it is my responsibility to take that into account.

Wisdom and folly are polar opposites. Being foolish means ignoring the facts, the counsel of wise people, or the lessons of history. Proverbs 15:2 says, "The tongue of the wise commends knowledge, but the mouth of fools gushes folly." Wisdom is shown by how one talks and acts.

> *Wisdom calls aloud in the street, she raises her voice in the public squares . . . Blessed is the man who finds wisdom, the man who gains understanding, for she is more profitable than silver and yields better returns than gold. She is more precious than rubies; nothing you desire can compare with her.*
> Proverbs 1:20; 3:13-15

Another definition of wisdom is, "the act of learning how to succeed in life."[3] The ancient philosophers viewed wisdom as "a philosophical study of the essence of life."[4]

Wise people will find that others seek their insight and counsel. In the history of nations, the wise advisers to kings and presidents truly wielded power. When a leader chooses fools as his counselors, disaster is imminent.

The Power of Spiritual Influence
Spiritually minded people wield power. First a small caution. Being spiritual does not make one knowledgeable in all areas of life. A spiritual person may be completely incompetent in matters of law, medicine, or finances. True wisdom will encourage counsel with people of expertise.

To possess spiritual influence one must be spiritual. The

question is, "What does it mean to be spiritual?" It means to be a committed follower of Jesus and to demonstrate that commitment by knowledge of the Scriptures, personal discipline, and appropriate action. Spiritual people grow in maturity. They show depth of life and understanding that has to do with the insight and wisdom described above.

People of spiritual influence do not lose influence when they lose their jobs or positions. They are not people of prejudice or hardened opinions. They are not swayed by public opinion. A person with spiritual influence has one of the most significant and powerful types of influence one can possess. When we combine in our own lives the powers of wisdom and character with spiritual influence, our words and actions begin to take on more significance.

Yet spiritual influence is something few people value—either to possess or to access. We are too often impressed with the most visible and tangible influences; we do not consciously seek spiritual influence.

Now that we have some definitions of power, let's ask some questions: Did Bruce possess power? Did the power he had satisfy him? Did Colonel Jack Swenson possess power? I leave that for you to consider.

More importantly, what kind of power do you desire? Try this exercise:

1. List the types of power you currently wield.

2. List the three or four types of power you value most.

3. List the three or four types of power you believe of highest value to God and to your family.

4. Compare the lists to see where you need to grow or develop.

WHERE DOES POWER ORIGINATE?

The obvious answer to this is God, the Creator. We are bound to the mind, body, abilities, heritage, and circumstances that God ordered by our birth. So in that sense, all power is from God.

Is there any power that is illegitimate? All power can be used for good or evil. This can even be said of God-given spiritual gifts and abilities. Whether or not we believe in royalty, dictators, or masters over slaves, when a society or culture permits these authorities, the person in authority or power has a choice to use it well. The kings of Israel and Judah in the Old Testament show how the entire nation suffered or prospered from the evil or good character of its leader. When one has power of any kind, it must be used well.

Let me propose another definition of power or a powerful life: People have power when they go through life meeting every circumstance, good or bad, with confidence and dependence on God. They arrive at their older years with the conviction that they have lived life well, with few regrets; that they used their gifts, power, and time for good and for God, serving their family and neighbors with selflessness and generosity.

Power does relate to how we meet, over time, the circumstances of life in the midst of chaos and complexity.

Paul speaks with wisdom and authority to those in the throes of suffering, difficulties, and human frailty: "If you only look at *us,* you might well miss the brightness. We carry this precious Message around in the unadorned clay pots of our ordinary lives. That's to prevent anyone from confusing God's incomparable power with us" (2 Corinthians 4:6-7, MSG). People should see power in us, but that power should be recognized as coming from God. It grows as we use to the fullest the gifts God has given us.

Many people of the past have commented on the concept of power. Some of these help us understand its blessings and dangers.

✖ Power corrupts, and absolute power corrupts absolutely. (Lord Acton)

✖ Nearly all men can stand adversity, but if you want to test a man's character, give him power. (Abraham Lincoln)

✖ Money is the most egalitarian force in society. It confers power on whoever holds it. (Roger Starr)

✖ The power of man has grown in every sphere, except over himself. (Sir Winston Churchill)[5]

When we get power, will it be of the right kind? Will we use it well?

In my study of Scripture, I see four primary elements that lead to a powerful life from God. Each of these four elements builds (as we say in mathematics and science) a "necessary and sufficient" foundation for a life of power. In the following chapters we will see how each one fits into the whole of making sense out of chaos.

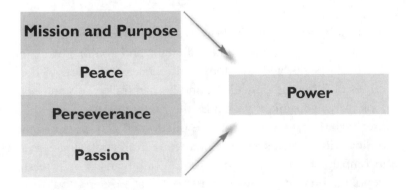

CHAPTER 6

MEANING AND PURPOSE

No one wants to live a meaningless and purposeless life. Every man and woman wants his or her life to be significant, to count for something. Depression, despair, and suicide are the results of life without meaning, life without reason to live. We feel great sadness when we see young people destroying their lives with drugs and alcohol. We grieve for people walking through life driven only by amusement, excitement, and thrills. We are dismayed when we observe people driven by peer pressure, lacking direction and motivation on their own.

We feel the same sadness when we walk through an urban area and see the helplessness of men and women caught in a web of culture and circumstances from which there is little escape. As we hurry by, we see homeless people and wonder who they were, who they are now, and who they will become.

If you have never visited a homeless shelter, you should. I spoke at a fundraising dinner for one of the best of these missions where they showed me their facility and programs. I saw families that had no place to go and no money. Many residents were abandoned. They were needy, enslaved to destructive habits, and in the iron grip of unfortunate circumstances.

But just as sad is seeing men and women giving themselves to purposes that have little meaning and that lead to poverty of spirit. They may be wealthy. They may have acclaim and public recognition. They may be admired and envied. But their lives are meaningless and unhappy.

We meet people daily who have a determined purpose, but little meaning. They have goals that drive them, but they find reaching these goals an empty experience. If you have ever climbed a mountain, you know the feeling of struggling up one arduous incline only to find, on reaching its crest, that another one immediately confronts you.

I'm not speaking against having goals—intermediate or long term—but simply want to point out that some goals can be wrong. An executive once said, "I clawed my way to the top of the ladder—only to find that the ladder was leaning on the wrong wall!"

Before we commit to life goals, we need to ask ourselves some questions:

✖ What do I want in life?

✖ What do I want in the process of walking through life?

✖ How will my goals affect the people in my life?

✖ Will my goals help others or hinder them from reaching their own goals?

We want to become more useful, more skillful, more confident, and more competent. Most of us sincerely want to mature emotionally, to develop intellectually, and to grow spiritually. We do not want to stagnate and become people of the past, or "has-beens." We do not want to live only in the memory of the past. We do not want to curl up in a corner and let the world go by.

The complexity and chaos of life keep us off balance. Just when we think we have life under control, a new set of problems enters to disturb us.

The words of a song express it well:

Why do new waves of trouble keep pounding around me
before yesterday's waves ebb away?[1]
"There's a Reason," Dan Foster

Did we really expect a pain-free, trouble-free life? Soon after our teenage years, our dreams begin to shatter. As much as we would like, we cannot escape it.

What keeps us going with resolve and even pleasure? It is *meaning* and *purpose*. Meaning and purpose provide a force, a motive, a determination to face life and to bring significance and accomplishment to every day. How do we derive true meaning and purpose? As unique and complex individuals, we must seek meaning and purpose particular to us.

We cannot normally pursue meaning and purpose in isolation. Most of us have family, friends, and coworkers for whom we are responsible. How many marriages have broken when one of the members simply says, "I don't know who I am. I need to find myself." The sad thing is that they seldom find themselves, often entering another relationship that also disappoints. In the guise of seeking true life-meaning, innocent lives are shattered.

On a recent writing vacation, I started every morning with a coffee latte and an apple turnover. I know, not exactly healthy food! On two mornings I encountered a couple in their fifties also beginning their day with lattes. Their bodies were covered with tattoos. Rings pierced their ears, noses, and lips, and their language was excessively foul. They were '60s hippies who had never changed. I can only imagine what their life had been—drugs, alcohol, and pursuit of freedom. I wondered what their dreams had been, how they now felt, and whether anyone now befriended them. They bore the outward marks of rebellion of an earlier time. Their earlier purpose had shattered their physical beings and left them outwardly damaged. I wish I could have asked what their meaning and purpose were now.

Most of us have been inward rebels, which does not leave physical marks. We desperately need to connect with meaning and purpose that satisfy for a lifetime through all the storms of chaos.

THE PITFALLS

The pursuit of real meaning and purpose has many pitfalls and detours:

Expecting a quick fix. From chapter 4 we know there is no quick fix for discovering meaning and purpose. It will take significant time and effort to discover and develop them.

Giving up. It is easy to quit. For instance, if we diet, we must exercise effort and discipline to achieve our goal. Then when the quest to lose weight becomes onerous, most of us quit. Similarly, in seeking to discover our meaning and purpose, to avoid the hard work required we adopt someone else's purpose and plan, only to find that it does not fit us. So we give up.

Withdrawing. Some of us withdraw from people and God and resort to living day by day with no plan or purpose. We become a world unto ourselves—a hermit in the urban neighborhood. Simon and Garfunkel wrote movingly about this: "I touch no one and no one touches me." [2]

Not doing "first things first." The practice of first things first is one of the most powerful self-management principles. This is a difficult discipline to apply. We are constantly sidetracked by secondary activities—opening junk mail, reading frivolous magazines, playing computer games, clearing our desks, watching television, and indulging other low-priority pursuits. To establish a sense of life direction, we must commit to doing first things first.

Not rebuilding shaky or cracked foundations. I would make a poor builder or contractor. My definition of a workshop project is one that can be started and finished in one evening. In our neighborhood the soil contains a type of clay called bentonite. With moisture it expands up to 15 percent. If a house's foundation is not properly prepared with several feet of nonexpanding fill to shield it from the bentonite, the foundation cracks and leaks. Many homes near us were shoddily built and now have cracking and crumbling foundations. Before any repair, the foundations must be dried out, refilled, and then repaired. Then real building can take place.

Before seeking meaning and purpose in your life, you may need to repair or rebuild some shaky foundations in certain areas:

✖ In your marriage
✖ In your spiritual life
✖ In your character
✖ In your physical health
✖ In your emotional health

Take the time to rebuild and repair. This will be the first step to discerning meaning and purpose in your life.

FINDING MEANING AND PURPOSE IN THE MIDST OF CHAOS

I asked fifty adults ranging in age from twenty to sixty to finish this statement: "When I come near the end of my life I will be pleased if . . . "

Here are some of the responses:

✖ I have impacted others by the life I have led.
✖ I enjoyed my life and didn't look too much at the past or the future.
✖ I have been a loving, strong, caring husband and father.
✖ I have peace about my life choices.
✖ I have left my family in good financial and emotional shape.
✖ I am remembered as a godly woman, wife, mother, grandmother, and neighbor. I have a long way to go!

✖ I go through death well and finish well.

✖ My integrity is intact.

✖ I have made a difference.

✖ I have a happy marriage.

✖ I have enjoyed my life—really lived it.

✖ My kids and grandkids would make some life decisions based on "what would Grandpa do?"

✖ Somehow the hurts I have given others are healed.

✖ I have made it back into my son's life.

✖ Those I have hurt will forgive me.

✖ I can face loss, sickness, and pain with peace, confidence, and trust.

✖ I remained involved in people's lives to the end.

✖ I have close relationships with family and friends.

✖ Others are better because I lived.

✖ To see joy in small wonders every day; to be able to laugh.

✖ I have discernment and the opportunity to be an encouragement to our children and grandchildren.

✖ I learn to make my marriage work: that is, we learn to talk (communicate), to resolve problems, to give and receive love, to work together for shared goals.

Because most of those who wrote comments were spiritually minded, they said things like:

✖ I finish life as a godly person.

✖ I hear "well done, good and faithful servant."

✖ My family knows Jesus Christ and they are living godly lives.

✖ I leave a legacy of godliness.

✖ Others have been drawn to Christ because of me.

✖ I end my life still loving and walking with God.

✖ I have walked in the path God had for me.

It is interesting to note what was *not* said.

✖ There were few comments on career or work.

✖ There were no comments on personal achievements.

✖ There were no comments on personal wealth.

✖ There were no comments on possessions.

G. K. Chesterton once said, "There are two ways to get enough. One is to continue to accumulate more and more and the other is to desire less."

Part of the lack of comments in these areas could be attributed to this group being older on the average and also overtly spiritual. Many are still pursuing careers, are achieving some measure of success, and are involved in worthwhile life pursuits.

Yet ultimate desires are similar for religious and nonreligious people. In our somber and reflective moments we know that material and career successes are fleeting and far less important than they seem to be at the time. Most end-of-life goals involve family, marriage, and personal happiness.

When we respond to these questions, we tend to write what sounds good, not always what resides in our deepest desires. I think there are and should be statements like:

✖ I have accomplished satisfying career goals.

✖ I have reached my financial goals for my family.

✖ I am respected by my peers.

Although these may sound self-centered or worldly, they are what most of us feel at some point in life.

Take a few moments now to respond to the same query: Near the end of my life I will be at peace if

_____ .

Write what comes to your mind. Don't be so altruistic that your statements reflect only what sounds good. Be real.

There is one problem. These answers do not fully describe meaning and purpose. They describe some end situations that we imagine we would want. For most of us this is too far in the future—and "it doesn't put bread on the table."

Let me summarize this section and address the next by saying,

Meaning in the midst of chaos
is living
a life with purpose,
a life without regret

A LIFE OF PURPOSE

Purpose is "raison d'être"—a reason for being. It means a life of significance, a life of substance. Purpose is "something one intends to get or do; intention; aim, resolution; determination. The object for which something exists."[3]

A person with purpose always has an end in mind, a goal, a vision for the future. Purpose gives us something to live for.

Brad struggles with alcohol. He has battled it for thirty years, as did his father. That, combined with some other life events, caused him to tell me, "There's nothing to live for, no meaning." I suggested his children. He said, "Yeah, but that is just temporary. They'll soon be gone."

Having a clear purpose keeps us going when life gets complicated and difficult.

Purpose is closely aligned with personal significance. A definition of significance is "having or expressing a meaning; full of meaning." So we see that meaning, purpose, and significance are intricately related. I believe it is impossible to sort out purpose from the normal things we wish to accomplish in life—being a good husband or wife, being a good mom or dad, exercising our gifts and abilities in our work, reaching goals of education and employment, and developing our personal character and spiritual walk.

In determining meaning and purpose, there are two clearly different perspectives. The first is where God and spiritual matters have little or no relevance. For those who practice their religion in a primarily social or cultural manner, the Scriptures and spirituality fail to be a major part of their life. In this case, meaning and purpose have a philosophical foundation based on values such as the worth of a human life, service to mankind, obligation to family, cultural moral values, or simply, self-preservation. These are good aims. I would never be critical of those who form their meaning and purpose from them. If they do so with love of people and moral consistency, they become valued members of society and generally happy people. Almost all secular books and seminars on significance and success build on the premise of human potential and self-determination as fundamental to a purposeful life.

Do these methods work without an overt knowledge of God? Yes, because the vast majority of principles and values come directly from the Bible—or can be found there. Yet I would argue that these will not be ultimately fulfilling.

Principled people do not set out to hurt others, destroy their families, or cheat their employers or employees. To do those things is simply not good business or good life skills. Significance, meaning, and goals are the cornerstones of the teaching in most secular self-help and well-being literature.

Much religious writing and teaching in these areas draws heavily on such resources. The philosophical and moral foundations in the writings of Plato, Aristotle, and more recent thinkers and philosophers possess great insights into human nature and ways to think and live. Who has not drawn on the wisdom of Benjamin Franklin? He was not overtly religious. In America we constantly refer to the "founding fathers"—Jefferson, Adams, Washington, and others to validate the current debate on values. Yet they were not generally believers in the way we describe followers of Christ today.

Thus, useful statements of meaning and purpose can be crafted without a God-focus. I believe such statements will lack critical elements, and more importantly, will lack the spiritual power that only God can give. Therefore, my suggestions for the building blocks of meaning and purpose will depend on the Bible and its teaching.

The Westminster Catechism said it well: "The chief end of man is to glorify God and to enjoy him forever."[4] Even more importantly, the Bible says it too. The preacher of Ecclesiastes wrote, "Here is the conclusion of the matter: Fear God and keep his commandments, for this is the whole duty of man. For God will bring every deed into judgment, including every hidden thing, whether it is good or evil" (Ecclesiastes 12:13-14).

And in the letter to believers living in Corinth, Paul wrote, "Whatever you do, do it all for the glory of God" (1 Corinthians 10:31).

In all of life we face an eternal perspective—an ultimate accounting for all that we do. And there is a dynamic present perspective: "Our people must learn to devote themselves to doing what is good, in order that they may provide for daily necessities and not live unproductive lives" (Titus 3:14). The apostle James wrote, "Do not merely listen to the word, and so deceive yourselves. Do what it says" (James 1:22).

In following Jesus, the present and the future must synchronize. One without the other is empty.

At the very beginning of your search for meaning and purpose, God asks to be the primary motivator. God has a purpose for you and will reveal it to you.

God Has a Purpose for You

Many people wonder if there is purpose and meaning for their existence. The Bible says there is: "For it is God who works in you to will and to act according to his good purpose" (Philippians 2:13). "By his power he may fulfill every good purpose of yours and every act prompted by your faith" (2 Thessalonians 1:11).

One of the most poignant verses in the Bible relates to the summary of Israel's King David in Acts 13:36: "For when David had served God's purpose in his own generation, he fell asleep [died]." The bookends of life are birth and death. What comes between either fulfills a destiny or destroys a dream.

There is purpose to life. There is a purpose for every person. David was a man specifically appointed by God to be king—but not without incredible struggles and trouble. He was a godly man, but made many mistakes. In summarizing his life, it was not the battles won, the courage exhibited, or the leadership extended. It was simply that he fulfilled God's purpose for his life.

It is a noble goal for each one of us to serve God's purposes. But what are those purposes? They include loving God and our neighbor and living a righteous life. But there is more. We must do what God asks. We must follow His leading in every aspect of life.

Our choice is simple—to decide whether or not to seek and follow God's purpose. Many people fail to recognize that this is the way of wisdom and happiness. Joshua said to the people of Israel as they were about to enter the Promised Land, "Choose for yourselves this day whom you will serve" (Joshua 24:15).

GOD'S GOAL

God has a purpose for each of our lives. Even if we are now following God, there is much that we have yet to explore. God also has a goal focus. The goal is specific.

Our ultimate goal is to please God: "So we make it our goal to please him, whether we are at home in the body or away from it" (2 Corinthians 5:9). Pleasing God, like pleasing one we love, is simply to obey and to do what He asks us to do. But we often resist. Most of us do not want to be told what to do—whether by children, husbands, wives, or employers. Obedience goes against human nature. Yet it is the way of love.

Reaching a goal takes work. As Paul wrote, "I press on toward the goal to win the prize for which God has called me heavenward in Christ Jesus" (Philippians 3:14). To please one's husband or wife requires constant attention, because our natural response always edges toward selfishness. To please God requires a focus and plan to do His will. Scriptures teach that human effort alone cannot please God.

"Are you so foolish? After beginning with the Spirit, are you now trying to attain your goal by human effort?" (Galatians 3:3). After once receiving God's salvation we cannot attain acceptance with Him by performing a series of religious acts to be more acceptable.

Human effort is required to live a godly life—in the power of the Holy Spirit. We do, and must, make choices and take action. Once we discover God's purpose for us, we must set goals to accomplish it.

FOCUS

In describing his life, Paul simply states, "But one thing I do: Forgetting what is behind and straining toward what is ahead, I press on toward the goal" (Philippians 3:13-14). There must be a compelling focus in our lives. Many parents of grown children watch children lose focus—change college majors, change jobs, change direction, fail to plan, ignore specific goals. This is the ethos of today's culture.

Former President John F. Kennedy pledged to place a man on the moon in the decade of the 1960s. I was part of that incredible momentum. It was a heyday of unrestrained technological experimentation and discovery. Since the end of World War II, no single grandeur so focused the efforts of our nation as landing a man on the moon. And we did it.

The power of focus on goals—and in some cases, on one significant goal—is incredible. A goal is not worth the paper it is written on without the focus to pursue it. Without vigorous effort, we revert to our myths, pipe dreams, and fairy tales.

We attend seminars, read books, and make pledges hoping to improve our lives—hoping to claw our way through our chaos, only to find ourselves once again without focus and commitment to a meaningful goal. Very little will happen without intensive focus. Follow-through, concentration, direction, and effort are all needed. Although human effort is not the major means of finding and deepening meaning, it is clearly a part of God's plan.

FOUNDATIONS FOR MEANING AND PURPOSE

What is the basis for meaning and purpose? How can I be happy and satisfied in life? Many people pursue this seemingly elusive state of mind and life through money, position, power, drugs, sex, adventure, or possessions. These things do not bring happiness and personal satisfaction. They often bring just the opposite—unhappiness and profound dissatisfaction.

Writing in *The Futurist,* Alan Thein Durning, a senior researcher at the Worldwatch Institute, says,

> People living in the 1990's are on the average four-and-a-half times richer than their great-grandparents were at the turn of the century, but they aren't four-and-a-half times happier … Rather than making their owners happy, these things [cars, motor boats, home entertainment centers, and whirlpool baths] apparently engender severe nervousness. To protect their possessions, Americans spent more on private security guards and burglar alarms than they paid through taxes for public police forces … Indeed, social scientists have found striking evidence that high-consumption societies, just as high

> living individuals, consume ever more without achieving satis-
> faction. The allure of the consumer society is powerful, even
> irresistible, but it is shallow nonetheless.[5]

In the University of Chicago Survey of Personal Happiness, about 30 percent in 1996 responded to being "very happy," down from 32 percent and 34 percent in 1986 and 1976. Most such indices reflect a downward trend, and this was in spite of a near doubling in both gross national product and personal consumption experienced per capita (since 1957).[6] More money, goods, and consumption are not making us happier.

One sad commentary was made by Christine Onassis, daughter of one of the world's wealthiest men and step-daughter of Jackie Kennedy Onassis: "Happiness is not based on money. And the best proof of that is our family."[7]

The sobering fact is that we, believers and nonbelievers alike, still pursue this imaginary "good life" and hold it up to our children as the ideal. The editors of *Fast Company* addressed the question, "How much is enough?" They concluded,

> At some level, most of us know that "more" is not only a
> promise—it's also a promissory note that lays claim to
> our time, to our families, to our energy, and to our hearts.
> Ultimately, there is no single answer to the question "How
> much is enough?" Ceaseless striving is indelibly stamped
> into the American character. The American Dream—an
> old engine that's been installed in the new economy—
> says that we can have it all. The American Reality whispers
> that when you do get it all, you'll only want more.[8]

Again we ask ourselves, "What does make people happy?" Most serious and credible surveys in the secular context list items like:

- A loving family
- A contented family life
- Religious practice
- Communication with people
- Community gatherings
- Sports
- Creative pursuits

Durning puts it well:

> In the final analysis, accepting and living by sufficiency rather than excess offers a return to what is, culturally speaking, the human home: to the ancient order of family, community, good work and good life; to a reverence for skill, creativity, and creation; to a daily cadence slow enough to let us watch the sunset and stroll by the water's edge; to communities worth spending a lifetime in; and to local places pregnant with the memories of generations.[9]

You may notice the lack of the spiritual element in the previous quotes. That is often an ignored element in the social science realm, though much emphasis has recently been put on a vague "spirituality." When such questions are asked of those with deep religious beliefs and practices, they show a marked increase in satisfaction with family, personal life, marriage, and life in general.

I propose that the most basic foundation for a life with meaning and purpose grows out of a deep faith in Jesus Christ. Not just in God, but in Jesus. Jesus is far more than a pattern for good living from His teachings—though that certainly is significant. The Jesus of the Bible was not just a good man living a good life, founding a new religion. He is the Savior, the One who died for our sin, who was resurrected from the dead, and who now offers salvation to anyone who comes to Him in faith. This is reflected in 2 Corinthians 5:17-18: "Therefore, if anyone is in Christ, he is a new creation; the old has gone, the new has come! All this is from God, who reconciled us to himself through Christ."

This does not mean becoming more religious or going to church. It means going beyond a general acknowledgment of God, or even of Jesus, to activating a personal relationship with Christ. If this idea or language is puzzling or strange to you, let me encourage you to spend time reading the Bible, beginning with the gospel of John. I also encourage you to become involved in a small group of friends to read the Bible and discuss its implications for life.

Out of this foundation all other major building blocks of life—family, work, community—find their meaning. From this foundation comes the basis for discovering and establishing real meaning and purpose for life.

Steps to the Future

The following steps are practical suggestions for formulating your personal purpose. Please remember that you are unique. Your purpose does not need to meet anyone else's expectations.

Two basic purposes seem to be universal for the spiritually minded man or woman.

1. We want to love and serve God with all our heart, mind, and soul. This is reflected in both the Old and New Testaments of the Bible.

2. We must make our family a primary component of our purpose. Whether married or single, we all have family connections and responsibilities. In many surveys, family emerges as the greatest source of both happiness and regret. In deliberating on your purpose, your marriage and family occupy a prominent place.

Here is a very simple outline to approach determining your purpose. I urge you to make notes and to write out your thoughts. You may want to do this two or three times over the next few months, because this is not a trivial exercise. This should be done in conjunction with related suggestions in chapter 11.

1. Set aside half a day—four hours—where you will have little or no interruption.

2. Ask God for wisdom and insight as you think in this area. Read one or two of your favorite portions of Scripture (if you don't have a favorite, read Psalm 139).

3. Reflect on your apparent current purpose. It may help to jot down some of your major activities and active passions.

4. Reflect on this question: *In what way do I sense dissatisfaction with my life and current purpose?*

5. Write out what you think your primary purpose should be. This should relate to what you view as your gifts, abilities, and skills. You might consider an overall statement of purpose and then some secondary purposes related to the major areas of life:
   - Personal life
   - Spiritual life
   - Family
   - Work
   - Finances
   - Health
   - Responsibility to others

6. Explore these questions: *What chaos am I presently encountering that impacts fulfilling my purpose and giving me real meaning? Is it external? Is it internal?*

7. *What can I do to specifically refocus my life around my purpose?*
   ✘ Immediately?
   ✘ In a month?
   ✘ In six months?
   ✘ In a year?

From my engineering and mathematical background, I would call this an "iterative" process. You will not get this right in one attempt. You will need to cycle back to this several times over a period of months to make your purpose clear and practical. Also, if you are married, you cannot do it in isolation from your spouse. Don't come home one day and announce that you have quit your job and plan to open a hot-dog stand at a nearby lake so you can be close to your children in a relaxed atmosphere!

An excellent resource is *Halftime* by Bob Buford (Zondervan, 1997). His later book, *Game Plan* (Zondervan, 1999), is more specific in practical suggestions. Also, I will give more detailed help on this entire process. We all need meaning and purpose that will keep us going through the difficult times. When you have such a purpose, it will free you to make choices that you know will please God.

CHAPTER 7

INTERNAL CHAOS:
THE SEARCH FOR PEACE

PEACE ON EARTH; GOOD WILL TOWARD MEN.

This refrain, heard most often at Christmas, reflects the desire of every person in the world. Yet it never seems to come. World peace is as elusive as a wisp of smoke. Throughout the centuries, men and women have valiantly attempted to create world peace, yet they have always failed. No matter how much they believed it to be possible, the force of evil destroyed every attempt. Greed, lust for power, and hatred overcame every plan for peace.

Although we desperately long for a lasting peace in the world, we see that it will never come in a material or international sense. Peace on this earth, in this war-torn world, will come only with the return of Christ at the end of the age. At this point I can't resist a quote about world peace: "Peace is the brief glorious moment in history when everybody stands around reloading." [1]

Since 1901, the Nobel Peace Prize has been presented to dozens of men and women who have given their lives to bring harmony, understanding, justice, and human rights for all. In spite of their efforts, peace eludes us.

The refrain of "peace on earth" is little more than wishful thinking—a fantasy. It bears little resemblance to the harsh reality of life in this world. Wars, racial hatred, poverty, terrorism, and hunger devastate much of the planet. From a human standpoint, it seems hopeless. With all of our technological achievements and discussions of biology and physics, little has been achieved in terms of true peace.

No one wishes to live in the midst of conflict. At this writing about thirty wars are raging around the world. Technology, communication, and advances in creature comforts do not keep tribes and nations in accord with one another.

Just prior to World War I, world leaders and many religious leaders foresaw true world peace. They wished to build "heaven on earth," a millennial reign of peace. They had visions of feeding the world, eradicating hunger, and dispensing with war as an outmoded means of settling disputes. In chapter 2 this was reflected by T. Baron Russell, who predicted that war would become obsolete. How wrong he was! Perhaps he should have heeded movie mogul Sam Goldwyn's advice, "Never prophesy, especially about the future!"

World War I shattered the dreams. It was a horrible war costing many lives on both sides of the conflict. The ill-fated League of Nations was born out of the enforced armistice, crippled by the onerous application of reparations to be paid by the conquered countries. That plan sowed a deep hatred and ferment that soon erupted into World War II.

The United Nations was then formed to attempt what the League of Nations failed to do—to keep worldwide peace. Since World War II the United States has engaged in the Korean conflict, the Vietnam conflict, and hundreds of other smaller wars. Peace is elusive, at best, and impossible at most. Hunger, poverty, and violence still fill millions of people with daily dread and fear.

In the midst of all this turmoil, people still persistently

search for peace. Some human suffering has been alleviated. Some comfort has been given. But people are born, live, and still die. The "in between," which we call life, is a constant search for peace and happiness. We long for deliverance from anxiety and worry.

What is peace? What are we really looking for? Peace in the world? Certainly. But that runs a distant second to the most profound longing—*personal peace.* We long for an escape from anxiety and worry, to be assured of the daily necessities of food, home, and safety. We want the absence of conflict both in our families and in the world.

It would be simple to say that we can find peace only in a personal relationship with Jesus Christ. While that is true, many believers do not experience peace. Peace is not synonymous with salvation.

We measure peace not so much by our desperation or even true adversity, but by how well our present reality meets our expectations. For example:

* A little boy in Calcutta may only want a pair of shoes or some food.
* A Muslim woman may want just a little freedom.
* A Sudanese peasant may simply want the safety of tribal security.
* An American boy may want to have his divorce-torn family reunited.

In our diverse world, peace comes in many forms—hopefully aligning with our expectations. But most often, this peace is only temporary.

With medical advances, technological breakthroughs, and material improvements, we should make progress toward peace and happiness in the world. In some ways we see improvement. Present conditions offer both encouragement and discouragement.

The human condition is gradually improving, especially in the West. Medical and economic advances, such as those described earlier, are easing the burden of life for many. But conditions are deteriorating in many developing nations. Other parts of the world experience slow change.

The world condition is somewhat better, certainly materially improving. However, it is far from healthy, with wars, poverty, and injustice still engulfing so many, with no foreseeable relief.

The American national condition—there is great debate on the American condition. There is little question that materially and economically we are steadily improving. The moral condition is deteriorating, gradually moving away from historic Judeo-Christian values and morality.

But *the personal condition* is another matter. As life externally becomes easier, does it become more peaceful and happy? Do shorter work hours and greater personal freedom for both men and women lead to peace? As believers, we would say, "No." But what would people in general say?

Social scientists do not attempt to measure peace, but they have conducted many studies in regard to happiness. Dr. Mihali Csikszentmihalyi, a professor at Claremont University, led the longest study of human happiness ever conducted. Of his many observations and conclusions, these stood out:[2]

✖ Though real average income doubled between 1964 and 1999, the measured level of happiness has remained the same.

✖ The happiness of high executives did not differ from that of the ordinary worker.

✖ Executives were more happy at work, less at home. Ordinary workers were happier at home, less at work.

✖ Children of suburban, higher-income families were not the happiest. Boys were bored and apathetic. Girls were anxious.

This study shows that happiness does not increase in a technologically advanced culture. In a telling final quote in his *Wall Street Journal* interview, Dr. Csikszentmihalyi discusses the ideal self, or "quantum self" as he calls it:

> It is about the notion that what you are experiencing now is not the ultimate—that you are a part of something that is much more interesting and complex than your own personal life. So you do the best to get the most out of what you have, but don't feel that that is the end ... sooner or later we have to jump from the notion of the self as revolving around our particular finite physical existence to consider ourselves as part of a much larger process of which we are a kind of temporary manifestation.[3]

He reflects what the Bible so clearly teaches—that we find a greater happiness in serving others, meeting their needs, than in focusing inwardly on our own selfish interests: "Do nothing out of selfish ambition or vain conceit, but in humility consider others better than yourselves. Each of you should look not only to your own interests, but also to the interests of others" (Philippians 2:3-4).

Another extensive study, *American Attitudes,* was recorded by Susan Mitchell in "The American Consumer Series." She found that people's self-assessment of their happiness significantly decreased from 1976 to 1996. The greatest decrease was among people under age thirty-nine.[4]

I share this to present facts, not just my narrow opinion, to the conclusion that peace and happiness are not increasing with time, but may well be decreasing. These studies were American, not reflecting other cultures and countries; but one thing is clear for every culture—everyone wants inner and outer peace and a measure of what they consider happiness.

We know little of how to measure happiness. Even in the

detailed *American Attitudes* study, the categories were simply: "Very happy, pretty happy, not too happy." Happiness, and even peace, are subjective and individual.

Human spiritual beings can experience the deepest of peace in the midst of incredible sorrow and unhappiness. With the wise man of Proverbs we say, "Even in laughter the heart may ache" (Proverbs 14:13).

The first time I used that verse with reality was in the midst of my personal sorrow. Our son, Steve, had been murdered just five weeks earlier. I was being given a going-away dinner at Hanscom Air Force Base, Massachusetts, where I had served as the reserve assistant to the commander for three years. There were gifts, jokes, and laughter common to such events, but with the heavy knowledge of what had happened to our family.

As I spoke in a farewell response, I said,

> Thank you for your kind words of condolence and for your friendship these three years. I think of a Bible verse that reflects Mary's and my thoughts. Proverbs 14:13 says, "Even in laughter the heart may ache." We do ache. We also reflect on another verse—my translation: "It is better to go to a funeral than to a banquet. For death is the end of every man, and the wise man will see it and learn" (Ecclesiastes 7:2). And yet we learned in this time more about peace than we learned through all our good times. It became "the peace that passes all understanding." With the chaos that entered our lives, I set out on this deeper search for the meaning of peace. So, we are learning and growing in this time of grief.

Everyone wants peace. The historian H. G. Wells wrote plaintively, "The time has come for me to reorganize my life, my peace—I cry out. I cannot adjust my life to secure any fruitful peace. Here I am at sixty-four, still seeking peace. It is a hopeless dream."[5]

Anne Morrow Lindbergh, in her classic book *Gift from the Sea,* wrote,

> I want first of all—in fact, as an end to these other desires—to be at peace with myself. I want a singleness of eye, a purity of intention, a central core to my life that will enable me to carry out these obligations and activities as well as I can. I want ... to live "in grace" as much of the time as possible. I'm not using this term in a strictly theological sense. By grace I mean inner harmony, essentially spiritual, which can be translated into outward harmony. I'm seeking perhaps what Socrates asked for in the prayer from the Phaedrus when he said, "May the outward and the inward man be as one." I would like to achieve a state of inner spiritual grace from which I could function and give as I was meant to in the eye of God.[6]

She gives voice to what lies deep in my heart—as, I believe, what lies in yours. We want a peace so ingrained and felt that it permeates every crevice of our lives. It is a peace that cannot be manufactured and yet is attainable. It is resident at the core of our beings, yet brings about peace in our outer lives and relationships.

Have you ever looked at the face of an older man or woman—seeing beyond the cracks, wrinkles, and sagging of age? You instinctively know that one person has lived a hard, angry, and unhappy life. And you see another whose face and eyes reflect a peace and contentment that you long for.

It shows. We can't hide it, especially as we grow older. There is a definite fruit of peace that permeates all of our being. Its healthy roots transform the fruit and the flowers of our external life, marking everyone around us.

> *"Peace I leave with you; my peace I give you. I do not give to you as the world gives. Do not let your hearts be troubled and do not be afraid."*
> John 14:27

What is this peace? How do we define it?

- Is it the absence of conflict?
- Is it the ability to endure and even prosper in complexity and chaos?
- Is it a "head in the sand" and "all will work out" mentality?
- Is it a withdrawal—a refusal to live with and face reality?
- Is it personal security? A selfishness that says, "I'm okay." After Hezekiah was healed of an illness by God, he was told of the calamities that would come on Israel. He selfishly replied, "'The word of the LORD . . . is good,' . . . For he thought, 'Will there not be peace and security in my lifetime?'" (2 Kings 20:19).
- Is it only a theological abstract—true, but not very practical?

Peace is none of these. Rather, true peace is a special peace that comes only from Jesus.

Peace is the gift of God, which is the fruit of true belief. The source of God's peace is in His Son, Jesus Christ. I use the phrase "true belief" because our use of *belief* is often weak. We believe in God. We believe Jesus was a good man—even the Savior. But there is a discontinuity between professed belief and changed lives. True belief should result in changed lives and external influence, even as it brings an inner peace. A result of inner peace should be expanded peace with family, friends, and coworkers.

> *"I have told you these things, so that in me you may have peace. In this world you will have trouble. But take heart! I have overcome the world."*
> John 16:33

A transaction of belief and faith must take place in our hearts to give the peace of which Jesus speaks. Conversion must take place. One of the evidences of this conversion is an inner peace—that knowledge that we are right with God.

This inner peace is deep and personal. It is evidenced in our hearts and minds. It is the "peace of God, which transcends all understanding" (Philippians 4:7). It is unmistakable when you possess it.

The Bible uses two rich words to describe peace. In the Old Testament the word for peace is *shalom*. It is used about two hundred times (three hundred fifty in various derivatives). Between fifty and sixty of these references explain the absence of strife. Almost two-thirds of the references show peace as the result of experiencing God's presence.

Psalm 4:8 says, "I will lie down and sleep in peace, for you alone, O LORD, make me dwell in safety." *The Message* phrases it, "At day's end I'm ready for sound sleep, for you, GOD, have put my life back together."

In the Old Testament, peace is strongly coupled with righteousness. One psalmist wrote, "Love and faithfulness meet together; righteousness and peace kiss each other" (Psalm 85:10). It is most clearly stated by the prophet Isaiah: "The fruit of righteousness will be peace; the effect of righteousness will be quietness and confidence forever" (Isaiah 32:17). There is no peace apart from righteousness: "Mark the perfect man, and behold the upright: for the end of that man is peace" (Psalm 37:37, KJV).

In the Old Testament, there was the *shalom* of the heart and the *shalom* of the community. God commanded His people to seek the *shalom* of the city or nation, such as Jerusalem. It meant to be whole, sound, or safe. According to Donald McGilchrist,

> Man brought peace offerings to God. Then, *shalom* is the situation where, due to God's goodness, everything can

flow in its own proper, undisturbed course to success. God moves to bring about *shalom*. It was often a synonym for what the Hebrews understood as salvation.[7]

In the Old Testament, there would be no *shalom* apart from righteousness—and no righteousness apart from obedience to God's commands and the sacrifice he demanded. All peace was first *with* God, then *to* man.

In the New Testament, the Greek word corresponding to the Hebrew *shalom* is *eivene*. It is used ninety times. This is a broad word, meaning well-being, restoration, reconciliation with God, and salvation in the fullest sense.[8]

> *I am the LORD your God, who knows what is best for you, who directs you in the way you should go. If only you had paid attention to my commands, your peace would have been like a river, your righteousness like the waves of the sea.*
> Isaiah 48:17-18

Jesus is the Prince of Peace—the ultimate shalom of Isaiah 9:6: "For to us a child is born, to us a son is given, and the government will be on his shoulders. And he will be called Wonderful Counselor, Mighty God, Everlasting Father, Prince of Peace."

God is called the God of peace: "The God of peace be with you all. Amen" (Romans 15:33).

The gospel is the "good news of peace through Jesus Christ" (Acts 10:36). Peace came *only* through Jesus. "Therefore, since we have been justified through faith, we have peace with God through our Lord Jesus Christ" (Romans 5:1).

TYPES OF PEACE

Several years ago Mary developed breast cancer. When I heard the word *cancer,* a chill ran down my spine. Immediately we stepped into a world of unknowns with all the questions anyone knows who has traveled down this road. How extensive is it? What kind of cancer? Is it contained? What is the prognosis? What are our options?

The cancerous lump was removed surgically, followed by radiation treatments. We embarked upon significant lifestyle changes in our diet. The surgeon told us he removed all the cancer and the radiation was precautionary. This should have brought about a lot of peace, calming our fears. But did it? We had several levels of peace during this time.

- We had *truth- or fact-based* peace. The surgeon said he got it all and the biopsy confirmed the truth.
- We reached *emotions-based* peace as we came to terms with the fact of cancer. Though we rode an emotional roller coaster, we soon settled into an emotional peace.
- Eventually we had an *experience-based* peace as Mary recovered and subsequent examinations revealed no cancer. Then after five years, the peace deepened in our hearts and minds.
- In the midst of the entire process we found it necessary and possible to believe that God was present with us in all of this and that He would do His will perfectly. This was *faith-based* peace.

This sequence demonstrates the various types of peace we encounter in life—and which we are taught in the Scriptures. One of the reasons we find peace so elusive is that we tend to use only one or two of these four dimensions as our measuring stick.

Truth-Based Peace

Truth-based peace comes from a foundation of the truth taught in Scripture. Much of the previous discussion related to truth. We first need to decide if truth resides in the Scriptures as the means God uses to communicate to us, rather than in some philosophical basis. Without that decision, the application of various passages of teaching from the Bible becomes meaningless. If we have entered into this eternal relationship with Jesus Christ, based on His death for our sin and His resurrection, then we do have *peace* with God. This is the sure teaching of Scripture. This is fact—or truth. Jesus is our peace.

Many professing Christians wrestle with their assurance of salvation, finding it difficult to simply accept God's statement of the truth. When I was young in my faith, I thought, "It can't be this simple. I must have to *do* something more than believe." I knew I had to live a good life, but I soon learned that living a good life could never earn salvation or peace with God.

As we navigate through our life with God, studying and understanding the truth of Scripture and what it teaches about salvation is imperative. I am always amazed at how much time people give to achieving competence in their professions, sports, and hobbies, and yet give so little time to understanding the most important relationship in life—a relationship with God. We must work on knowing the truth of the biblical and theological basis of peace with God.

Emotions-Based Peace

We are a people of emotions and feelings. Our feelings may not relate to reality, but more to current circumstances and relationships. Our emotions can never be the measure or barometer of our spiritual journey. Yet we long for an emotional peace.

God promises peace that "transcends all understanding" (Philippians 4:7). In the midst of great turmoil, God alone gives peace, which I define as the quiet confidence that I am secure in God's hands.

> *Lord, keep me still,*
> *Though stormy waves may blow*
> *And waves my little bark may overflow,*

Or even if in darkness I must go;
Lord, keep me still.

The waves are in Thy hand,
The roughest seas subside at Thy command.
Steer Thou my bark in safety to land
And keep me still,
Keep me still.

Author unknown

Many times in turmoil, I have experienced a gradual settling of peace in my emotional being.

It is not just troubles that disturb our emotional peace. Often it is the unsettledness of the direction of our lives and of our most valued relationships. I have seen my peace disappear over stresses and strains in my family. The relentless push for achievement and affluence will, in our quieter moments of reflection, disturb our emotional peace as we sense that we are giving ourselves to that which has little or no meaning.

Emotions-based peace is the most variable and unreliable peace, yet it is that which we most desire.

Experience-Based Peace

Growing older is both a blessing and a curse. With age comes experience—which can make us bitter and cynical or give us peaceful confidence. Children and teens become anxious and worried as they encounter life issues, largely because they have no context or experience to frame their situation.

Have you ever wondered why the Old Testament repeats the story of the great Exodus from Egypt so many times? It is explained in Deuteronomy 8:2: "Remember how the LORD your God led you all the way in the desert these forty years, to humble you and to test you in order to know what was in your heart, whether or not you would keep his commands." When the Israelites remembered what God had done in the past, they would, from experience, have courage to stay obedient to God.

We all know the glib phrase, "Been there. Done that." It says, "I have had that experience before and know what to expect."

David found himself in trouble many times. In Psalm 77 he reflects on one of those times.

> I cried out to God for help; I cried out to God to hear me ... I thought about the former days, the years of long ago; I remembered my songs in the night. My heart mused and my spirit inquired ... I will remember the deeds of the LORD; yes, I will remember your miracles of long ago. I will meditate on all your works and consider all your mighty deeds. Your ways, O God, are holy. (Psalm 77:1,5-6,11-13)

What was David doing? He was reviewing what God had done for him and for his people. From that he drew strength and hope. He was finding peace in his present troubles through his experience with God from the past.

When I have faced difficulties and peace was elusive, I looked back on my life, reviewing how God had worked in many circumstances.

- My parents' divorce when I was a baby and how God protected me.
- How God used a businessman and a student to introduce me to Christ.
- How I met Mary.
- How we reacted after a fire destroyed everything we owned.
- How good came after a life-changing failure.
- How all our Air Force assignments turned out for the best.

✖ How God supplied our finances when we joined The Navigators.

When I review these situations, it helps bring me back to an experience-based peace. I have been there before. I know it will work out.

Faith-Based Peace

Often we are in turmoil over decisions we must make or have made. Anxiety, not peace, comes crashing into our lives. In these times, we are forced to trust God—when we cannot control the outcome (which is most of the time). We reach peace when we finally leave it to Him—by faith.

Decisions allow us to *do* something. The more difficult situation is when we find ourselves in circumstances over which we have no control—death of a loved one, loss of a job, a divorce, rebellious children, or family tension.

Speaking about his personal suffering, Paul wrote, "I know whom I have believed, and am convinced that he is able to guard what I have entrusted to him for that day" (2 Timothy 1:12).

The apostle Peter reflected on unjust suffering saying, "So if you find life difficult because you're doing what God said, take it in stride. Trust him. He knows what he's doing, and he'll keep on doing it" (1 Peter 4:19, MSG).

Faith is a key element in all these dimensions. But there comes a time when truth, emotions, and experience do not suffice, and all that remains is faith. Faith in the right thing is imperative. Faith is not just a generic belief in some nebulous concept. It must be faith in a living, active God.

One of the most significant results of our peace is that we want to share this peace with others. Finding our peace in Christ suddenly lifts our eyes to people—real people, who have little or no access to the knowledge of Jesus. If our peace is real and firmly rooted in the gospel of Jesus, we become restless until we reach out to the lost of the world—both those who are near us and those in distant lands.

As I was reflecting on peace recently, I decided to call my friend Major General Ed Mechenbier. Ed now holds the same responsibility I once held in the Air Force Reserves. He is an Air Force Academy graduate and a fighter pilot. His story helps illustrate the dimensions of peace described above.

For five years, eight months, and four days, Ed was a prisoner of war in Vietnam. He had been piloting an F-4C on a bombing mission near Hanoi. He was shot down at precisely 2:15 P.M. on June 14, 1967—the American National Flag Day. I'll let Ed tell his story:

> When I was captured after bailing out of my damaged F-4C, they herded us through several villages, beating us, and bombarding us with stones. Then they stopped and lined us up by several graves. A firing squad raised their rifles, "Ready, aim ... oh, let's get some more pictures. Ready, aim ..." This was repeated five times. Just before the fifth time I lifted my eyes and saw a statue of the Virgin Mary on the hillside and somehow I knew I would be okay.
>
> I thought, "This is a good place to die. I am here for a reason. In fact, I won't die."
>
> Five months later I was in solitary confinement pacing the floor. Suddenly, in desperation, I said, "Jesus, if you're really with me, make this bunk move!" Then I thought, "I never would have said that if I didn't believe He was there. I don't need the bunk to move. He is here."

I asked him when he heard that he would be freed.
"On February 3, 1973, five days after the peace agreement."
"Did you believe it?"
"No. No way. It can't be true. More lies."
"When did you *begin* to believe it would happen?"

"It was on February 18, 1973, as we were transported to the airport and I saw an airplane with those familiar 'United States Air Force' markings. I thought, 'I hope it's real. I'm not out yet. Something could go wrong.'"

"When did you *really* believe it?"

"When the tires of the airplane broke ground from the runway in Vietnam. There was shouting, yelling, stomping feet up and down the aisles. We knew it was true!"

"When was the next point of peace and assurance?"

"When the pilot announced that we had left Vietnamese air space. Then the freedom took on reality in the Philippines as I wolfed down food like a kid in a candy store. With my first call home to the family and the incredible receptions both in Hawaii and California, I *knew* I was free!"

Peace comes slowly with the reality of the truth, the emotions of being freed, the experience of actually having the freedom. Its foundation is faith that takes root early on as we "walk by faith, not by sight."

Peace is the result of true freedom in Christ. It is not a theory based on hearsay. As Ed felt when the plane lifted off the runway in Vietnam, we need to experience the reality and have the peace deep in our hearts.

CHAPTER 8

Living Through Chaos

NOTHING IN THE WORLD CAN TAKE THE PLACE OF PERSIST-
ENCE. TALENT WILL NOT: NOTHING IS MORE COMMON
THAN UNSUCCESSFUL PEOPLE WITH TALENT. GENIUSES WILL
NOT: UNREWARDED GENIUS IS ALMOST A PROVERB.
EDUCATION WILL NOT: THE WORLD IS FULL OF EDUCATED
DERELICTS. PERSISTENCE AND A DETERMINATION ALONE ARE
OMNIPOTENT. THE SLOGAN "PRESS ON" HAS SOLVED AND
ALWAYS WILL SOLVE THE PROBLEMS OF THE HUMAN RACE.[1]

CALVIN COOLIDGE

*(The following classic speech, given by Winston Churchill
at Harrow School on October 29, 1941, ranks with the
shortest and most powerful speeches of all time.)*

NEVER GIVE IN, NEVER GIVE IN, NEVER, NEVER, NEVER — IN
NOTHING, GREAT OR SMALL, LARGE OR PETTY — NEVER
GIVE IN, EXCEPT TO CONVICTIONS OF HONOR AND GOOD
SENSE. NEVER GIVE IN.[2]

WINSTON CHURCHILL

THE NEED FOR PERSEVERANCE

The easiest thing in the world is to give up—to quit. The
hardest thing is to keep going when life seems hopeless. I

love watching the persistence of small children. "Dad, please. Can I have a candy? Please. I really want to." And on it goes. Hour after hour, day after day. When they set their minds on something, they are unstoppable. When they are little, we are amused, though a bit exasperated. As they grow, this persistence can be a source of incredible conflict.

Something happens to their persistence along the way to adulthood. For many teenagers, the drive and persistence dissipates. Or perhaps it is refocused on the wrong things. After life has buffeted us, bringing pain and disappointment, we easily lose the strength or desire to persevere.

When our daughters were in gymnastics, the phrase "when the going gets tough, the tough get going" was common. But we may respond, "I really do not want to be tough."

Sometimes we just wear down and lose our ability to keep up the motivation and persistence. I have personally been there a number of times. We wonder, *Is it worth it? Can I take the pain? Do I have the resilience to dig out of my emotional hole and keep trying?*

History, novels, and movies are filled with people who endure against all odds—athletes, politicians, ordinary people in extraordinary difficulty, soldiers, and martyrs. Tales of courage and endurance capture our imagination. Stories of Medal of Honor recipients (not winners—they did not enter a competition) stir the heart with deeds of unselfishness and bravery. When asked, most medal recipients simply respond, "I was just doing my duty."

Athletes provide many stories of perseverance. In the 1968 Olympics in Mexico City, one man's finish taught more than any gold medal.

THE GREATEST LAST-PLACE FINISH EVER
Out of the cold darkness he came. John Stephen Akhwari, of Tanzania, entered at the far end of the stadium, pain

hobbling his every step, his leg bloody and bandaged. The winner of the Olympic marathon had been declared over an hour earlier. Only a few spectators remained. But the lone runner pressed on.

As he crossed the finish line, the small crowd roared out its appreciation. Afterward, a reporter asked the runner why he had not retired from the race, since he had no chance of winning. He seemed confused by the question. Finally, he answered:

"My country did not send me to Mexico City to start the race. They sent me to finish."[3]

My heroes are those ordinary people who battle cancer, who work hard to give their children an education, who sacrifice their success to stand up for truth, who endure suffering at the hands of corrupt governments, and who resist bitterness when they are wronged.

One of my personal mentors and heroes was Bud Ponten, who had cerebral palsy. I observed his life for over thirty-five years as he endured and never gave up—even when work and life seemed hopeless. He taught me to play ping-pong and tennis. He showed me how to operate a hand-fed printing press. Most of all, he taught me courage and the love of God.

Glenn Cunningham was a young boy attending a rural Kansas school. He and his brother had the responsibility of starting the fire in the schoolhouse stove each morning. On a February morning in 1916, someone had accidentally filled the kerosene container with gasoline, and the stove exploded. Glenn's brother was killed and Glenn, age six, was severely burned. Doctors feared for his life. His legs were severely burned, leaving little hope of his ever walking again. The doctors recommended amputation. Glenn's mother could not bear that. She kept putting it off, continuing to help him. He spent weeks in bed. Then he slowly walked on crutches.

He said later, "It hurt like thunder to walk, but it didn't hurt at all when I ran. So for five or six years, about all I did was run."[4] Progress was slow but he persisted. In high school, Glenn set an interscholastic record of 4.27 minutes for the mile. At the University of Kansas, he competed in the 1,500-meter races, winning the NCAA title in 1932. He was the winner of the Sullivan Award, given to the nation's outstanding amateur athlete in 1933. He set the world record for the mile of 4.06.7 minutes in the Princeton Invitational Meet in 1933. In the 1932 Olympics he placed fourth in the 1,500-meter event. In 1936 he won a silver medal.

Glenn Cunningham had persistence and determination. Because the burns damaged his circulation, he needed to spend an hour preparing for each race—massaging his legs and then doing a long warm-up.

He retired from active competition in 1940. Despite his injuries, he spent two years in the Navy. He earned a master's degree and a doctorate. He and his wife opened the Glenn Cunningham Youth Ranch in Kansas, where they helped to raise ten thousand underprivileged children over a period of years. He was a lay preacher who acted on his faith.

Most of us don't become public heroes like Glenn Cunningham. But his example of endurance and persistence is valid for us all.

The Bible is filled with stories of men and women who persevered in life and faith: Esther, a commoner who became queen; Elijah, Jeremiah, Jonah—prophets who spent much of their lives on the run; and John, the exiled author of Revelation.

Paul encouraged his protégé Timothy to "keep your head in all situations, endure hardship, do the work of an evangelist, discharge all the duties of your ministry" (2 Timothy 4:5).

THE ANATOMY OF PERSEVERANCE

Perseverance has many faces. We tend to think only in terms of the big problems, the really difficult tasks, or massive suffering.

When we work out with weights in the gym, we know we must begin with small weights, gradually strengthening our muscles and increasing weight with time. We build perseverance in the same way. We learn to persevere in small matters and we are strengthened for future challenges.

Let's look at some synonyms to help us understand perseverance:

Endurance is the ability to last, to continue, to remain in whatever we are doing. Endurance in athletics paints a good picture. In my passion for handball, I need strength to hit the ball hard. I need energy from good nutrition to keep going. I have a bad habit of skipping breakfast or lunch, and sometimes both. Then at 4:15 P.M. I go into a handball court and become exhausted after fifteen minutes of hard play. I wonder why?! I also need "wind"—the ability to keep oxygen coming into my system through my heart, lungs, and blood. To be able to play a two-hour match without constantly gasping for breath takes weeks and months of preparation. Endurance relates to overall physical condition.

There is one last element that I find vital in handball. That is mental focus, concentration, accompanying the endurance—a mindset to keep going and not give up even if I am losing.

Persistence is what we often see with children. They keep pressing and pushing until they get their way. We need to persist—to decide to continue something in spite of opposition and difficulty. I like the story told of Cato, the Roman scholar. He "started to study Greek when he was over 80. Someone asked why he tackled such a difficult task at his age. 'It's the earliest age I have left,' said Cato . . . and went right on studying."

Tenacity is similar to persistence. It is hanging on doggedly no matter what obstacles we face.

Steadfastness is a biblical word. It comes from the Greek word *hupomeno,* meaning "patient enduring." In 1 Corinthians 15:58 we are told to be "steadfast, immovable" (ESV). The Bible speaks of our hope being "sure and steadfast" (Hebrews 6:19, ESV). Steadfastness will not fade or fail. It lasts forever.

Resolve, or resolution, means making a decision and keeping it as we pursue a specific direction. We need to *resolve* to *persevere.*

Other words could be used: firmness, stability, fortitude, courage, decisiveness, relentlessness. Each of these words captures a dimension of perseverance. In short, perseverance means to keep going, to remain faithful in the direction of God's call and will.

Barbara McClintock was a researcher in genetics. In the early 1940s she discovered the "jumping genes" in Indian corn. Her colleagues and the scientific community ridiculed her. Then in 1983 she was awarded the Nobel Prize in Physiology for her work. When she was eighty-five, she was asked in an interview, "How did you keep going when no one agreed with you?" She quietly said, "When you know you are right, you don't care what people think." She simply persisted in her research.

Other factors impact our ability to persevere. We are complex beings. There is no "one-size-fits-all" when it comes to how we respond to the circumstances of life. Personality, health, age, and history and experience all affect each person's response to situations that call for perseverance.

Personality
We are unique beings. God created us with distinct personalities. Some of these personality traits can be seen even in

babies of a few months of age. We often categorize people into four personality types—choleric, sanguine, melancholic, phlegmatic—but we are more complex than that. We may demonstrate a dominant type, but we see in ourselves blends of personality traits.

However we choose to talk about ourselves, we do know that personality determines much of how we respond in given situations. Some people are naturally stubborn, persistent, and aggressive. Others are more reflective, inward, and plodding in response. Still others may be less driven and more compliant. Some are highly motivated and goal-oriented. Others are relational and sensitive.

Your personality does make a difference. Therefore, it is helpful to recognize your own tendencies and personality. They will affect your personal response to issues that call for perseverance.

Health

Both physical and emotional health deeply affect how much perseverance we can exert at any point in time. By physical health I mean both your medical condition as well as your physical conditioning. If you are ill or suffer from a chronic medical condition, your physical endurance will be reduced. I am often amazed how my friends with cancer, migraine headaches, or other long-term illnesses cope and rise above their circumstances to endure and persevere in many areas of life.

One veteran missionary told me, "There are two kinds of missionaries. One is ill and everybody knows it. The other is ill and no one knows it. But everyone is ill." He served in areas that lacked sanitation and where tropical diseases were rampant. Perhaps those of us who are relatively healthy and have inherited strong physical constitutions get more discouraged and distracted by illness than those who have lived with limitations for many years.

Emotional health impacts our ability to function and endure as much as physical health. When we are "down" emotionally, we find perseverance a difficult task. Depression and other emotional disorders are not minor—they are intensely important in our overall health. Fatigue, extensive conflict, and chaotic schedules contribute to emotional debilitation and hinder even the strongest of us in persevering. Guard, and heal, your emotional self.

Age

As I grow older, endurance in many arenas has become more difficult. Obviously I do not have the physical stamina I had at age twenty-five. I also tire more quickly of conflicts in work and personal life. I note my tendency to avoid problems rather than solve them. I find myself becoming more impatient—even irritable at times, though Mary tells me it does not show externally. In some ways my inner energy level is stronger. I know some people who, as they get older, become less mentally agile and find it harder to focus on several problems at once.

With age *can* come strength of inner character, which leads to perseverance when principles and integrity are at stake. With age, there is less to lose by way of reputation and, thus, there is more courage to speak one's mind. Patience, in one sense, is easier because you have seen a process or pattern in the past and intuitively know its outcome. On the other hand, impatience may also be present for the same reason.

On the negative side of age, we may lose the heart or drive to battle through difficult issues and problems. We may want to throw our hands up and say, "Who cares?" when we most need to keep going.

Whether positive or negative, age becomes a key factor in perseverance. A caution: age and seniority do not make a person wiser or more godly. The Bible says, "Better a poor but wise youth than an old but foolish king who no longer knows how to take warning" (Ecclesiastes 4:13). An older man or woman can be as foolish as any young person. If character and godliness have not been the foundation of one's life, simply having gray hair or secular experience will not ensure any level of wisdom. But it is never too late. God wants to develop our character and relationship with Him no matter what our chronological age.

History and Experience

"A prudent man sees danger and takes refuge, but the simple keep going and suffer for it" (Proverbs 22:3). Experience and history are wonderful teachers. Together they exert a powerful influence over every area of life. Personal experience and history, combined with the experience and history of others whom we have understudied or known, form a foundation of mental and emotional reserves that profoundly influences our responses. Every circumstance we encounter automatically flashes pictures and feelings of the past on our mental video screens. They bring either fear or courage, depending on the past. They cry out to us to "give up!" or "keep going!"

Have you seen or known people who have been so beaten down by life that they are incapacitated—almost incapable of rational action? We see this often among the homeless, clients of rescue missions, urban single moms, and the poor. It seems so simple and obvious to those who are strong and successful to tell them to "buck up" and to "make something of yourself." We know that does not work—and it may not even be possible. But the same thing happens to us internally; our history and experience debilitate us from having perseverance and endurance.

PAUL'S PERSONAL EXPERIENCE OF PERSEVERANCE

The apostle Paul was a man born to battle and to a life of pressures and difficulties. Before he became a believer in

Jesus, he was scouring the country for Christians whom he could throw in prison. He was present at the stoning of Stephen, giving his approval. He was a man on the move to higher positions in the Jewish establishment.

Then Paul (called Saul before his conversion) encountered Jesus on the road to Damascus. First he was blinded by a light. Then Jesus spoke to him, "Saul, Saul, why do you persecute me?"

"Who are you, Lord?" Saul asked.

"I am Jesus whom you are persecuting" (Acts 9:4-5).

If Paul thought he was a mover and shaker before, he was now entering a life where his earlier adventures would seem like child's play. After his conversion, Paul became the primary missionary to the Gentiles, walking in the eye of the storm most of his life.

Later Paul was called upon to defend himself. Many believers in these early days of Christianity were being persecuted. Paul relates his hardships:

> Are they servants of Christ? (I am out of my mind to talk like this.) I am more. I have worked much harder, been in prison more frequently, been flogged more severely, and been exposed to death again and again. Five times I received from the Jews the forty lashes minus one. Three times I was beaten with rods, once I was stoned, three times I was shipwrecked, I spent a night and a day in the open sea, I have been constantly on the move. I have been in danger from rivers, in danger from bandits, in danger from my own countrymen, in danger from Gentiles; in danger in the city, in danger in the country, in danger at sea; and in danger from false brothers. I have labored and toiled and have often gone without sleep; I have known hunger and thirst and have often gone without food; I have been cold and naked. (2 Corinthians 11:23-27)

Reread this passage slowly, putting yourself in each of these situations. How would you have responded? Would you have kept going? What are your limits?

We may think that Paul was a special person, a super-man called to save the world. He was just like us. Certainly he had a call from God. But so do we. Some of us have a personality like Paul's—driven, directed, blunt, and active. Or we may be his polar opposite, like Timothy. Paul possessed no more resources than we do. He had to decide how to act and live in his circumstances, both good and bad. He commented, "I have learned to be content whatever the circumstances. I know what it is to be in need, and I know what it is to have plenty. I have learned the secret to being content in any and every situation, whether well fed or hungry, whether living in plenty or in want" (Philippians 4:11-12).

Learning the Secret

Paul discovered a secret and applied it to his life. On a recent flight, I was seated next to a young businesswoman. She had just been reading a self-help article in a magazine. Then I noticed she wrote down on her pad: "What do I want to be? To work toward? What do I really think and feel?"

I have done that. Most of us have. We wonder how to take the next step in our lives. To overcome disappointment. To make something of ourselves. To have meaning. It drives all of us, though we may never write it down.

But what are our resources to do these things? All the self-help books in the world (including this one) will not give the answer. It must come from God and from deep within ourselves. We work to discover that "secret" that puts it all together and unlocks the future.

Let's examine three aspects of Paul's secret, from his writings:

1. Christ gives me strength for everything I must do. "I can do everything through him who gives me strength" (Philippians 4:13). That is such a simple statement underlying such a big truth. The truth: Jesus gives us strength.

2. It is strength for *everything* I do. "Yeah, yeah . . . a good sermon. But I need something practical, something that works—now!"

Let me ask: To what degree have you tried Jesus? Jesus, or the name of Jesus, is not some magic word that you repeat as a mantra and a miracle happens. Nor is Jesus a man-servant who appears at your side saying, "And what may I get for you now?"

When Paul said he could do everything through Christ, he spoke of an indwelling Jesus who gave him salvation and who daily spoke with him and led him. The "salvation" pill of "receiving Jesus" in some cavalier way is not enough. There must be surrender to the complete salvation He offers. It involves submission to Jesus in salvation, which begins to change how we think and live. Our tendency is to "believe in Jesus," and then go on to conduct our lives in pretty much the same way we did before. There must be a conscious decision to depend on the strength Jesus offers.

Through the years I have tried dozens of ways to keep myself physically fit—often for two rather questionable results: appearance and better handball! I wish I could say that it was always to glorify God! On my better days, that is my motivation.

Here is my pattern. Something happens—such as becoming ill, gaining weight, or performing badly on the handball court. I resolve to "do something about it." I then find some regimen of nutrition and exercise that someone tells me will work. It works well—for three weeks. Then I slip back to old patterns. What I fail to realize and practice is that there are only a few necessities—diet, exercise, and consistent practice. It takes self-discipline, perseverance, and some level of motivation.

Finding strength in Jesus is similar. We need a basic diet of spending time with Him regularly in the Scriptures and prayer. We must exercise a commitment to do what He tells us. Then we must keep doing that even when we don't feel like it, when we don't feel the need, or when we're too busy.

We also must practice what we believe. Then strength (power) is experienced. I can daydream all I want about how to have a stronger, faster shot in handball, but until I spend time with some weights in the exercise room, it will never happen.

In the spiritual realm,

- I need to believe that I can get all the strength I need from Jesus, and
- I need to practice living in His strength every day.

3. When difficult times come, I need to persevere. The ability to persevere comes from the "power from God," which Paul wrote about in 2 Corinthians 4. Here is how Paul described his responses:

- *Hard pressed on every side, but not crushed.* As the saying goes, he was "up to his armpits in alligators." He saw no way out. *But* he could not be crushed. He knew from truth he had learned and from personal experience that God would sustain him.
- *Perplexed, but not in despair.* At times he could not figure out what was happening to him—or why. He was perplexed, confused, *but* he would not permit himself to give up in despair. Many times we must keep going when we have no clue as to the root of our problems and circumstances.
- *Persecuted, but not abandoned.* Not many of us in the West today have really been persecuted, even though we may feel like we are on the receiving end of persecution. However, in our world today, many people actually do suffer persecution for their faith. *But* we have the absolute

confidence that we are not orphaned—not abandoned. God is still there, watching out for us.

✖ *Struck down, but not destroyed.* There are setbacks, hard times, illnesses, great disappointments—but they *will not* destroy us.

✖ Finally, Paul simply said, "Therefore we do not lose heart. Though outwardly we are wasting away, yet inwardly we are being renewed day by day"
(2 Corinthians 4:16).

When you read Paul's writings, you do not see a man who had it all figured out. You see a man in process, wrestling with the circumstances of life and, under the inspiration of the Holy Spirit, writing what he discovered.

How did Paul cope with all his trials? What caused him to want to keep going—to not quit? Was it simply gutsy perseverance? He tried to express it in 2 Corinthians 6:3-5:

> We put no stumbling block in anyone's path, so that our ministry will not be discredited. Rather, as servants of God we commend ourselves in every way, in great endurance; in troubles, hardships and distresses; in beatings, imprisonment and riots; in hard work, sleepless nights and hunger.

These were the negatives—the context. Now comes the "how" (verses 6-7):

in purity	This is purity of life and motive.
[in] understanding	Understanding of the Scriptures, of God, and of his circumstances.
[in] patience	Waiting for God to work.
[in] kindness	Kindness is an issue of character as well as a decision to treat people well.

in the Holy Spirit	Paul's patience, kindness, purity, and understanding were not inherent in his human nature, but dependent on the Holy Spirit who dwelt in him and guided him.
in sincere love	This spoke of his inner motive—love for people and love for God.
in truthful speech	Paul insisted on proper, godly communication. "Speaking the truth in love, we will . . . grow up into Him" (Ephesians 4:15).
in the power of God	Again, not in Paul's own power. He did not persevere in a self-imposed discipline. He relied on God's power.
with weapons of righteousness in the right hand and in the left	This description is reflective of Paul's teaching in 1 Corinthians 10:4: "The weapons we fight with are not the weapons of the world. On the contrary, they have divine power to destroy strongholds." We are in a spiritual battle. Satan wants us to give up, to admit defeat.

This long list shows the complexity of a single idea—perseverance. It shows that perseverance and endurance have deep spiritual roots in our relationship to Christ.

I have spent most of my life attempting to live in a way that pleases God. In that journey I have experienced a significant amount of what the world would call "success." Also on the journey I have become much more aware that God wants to deeply change my character. He is far more interested in *who I am* than in *what I do.* As I have reviewed my life, I cannot say that I developed in any significant way in my successes. God brought the growth almost exclusively in times of difficulty and suffering. I don't like this observation. I wish there were easier ways to grow in character.

I tried to lay good foundations. I studied the Scriptures. I worked on personal obedience. I knew the biblical theology. But inner growth came as I walked through hard times and as

I learned what it meant to endure and persevere. Unfortunately, I know that I am still a student—a man on the way. Yesterday's victories do not ensure today's godly walk. "He knows the way that I take; when he has tested me, I will come forth as gold" (Job 23:10).

> Contrary to what might be expected, I look back on experiences that at the time seemed especially desolating and painful with particular satisfaction. Indeed, I can say with complete truthfulness that everything I have learned in my seventy-five years in this world, everything that has truly enhanced and enlightened my existence, has been through affliction and not through happiness. In other words, if it ever were to be possible to eliminate affliction from our earthly existence by means of some drug or other medical mumbo jumbo, as Huxley envisaged in *Brave New World,* the result would not be to make life delectable, but to make it too banal and trivial to be endurable. This, of course, is what the Cross signifies. And it is the Cross, more than anything else, that has called me inexorably to Christ.[5]
>
> Malcolm Muggeridge

CHAPTER 9
_____

THE FOUNDATION OF PERSEVERANCE

IF GOD PROMISED HIS SERVANTS AN UNBROKEN RUN OF
PROSPERITY, THERE WOULD BE MANY COUNTERFEIT
CHRISTIANS. DON'T BE SURPRISED AT FAMINE ...IT IS PER-
MITTED TO ROOT YOU DEEPER JUST AS A WHIRLWIND
MAKES THE TREE GRAPPLE DEEPER ROOTS INTO SOIL.[1]

F. B. MEYER

Truth, especially biblical truth, is like sand or oil. Like sand it grinds at us, smoothing the rough places, causing friction in our moving parts to get our attention and to halt certain directions. Like oil, truth can smooth the rough ways of life, soothe the hurts, and even heal the brokenhearted.

Learning biblical truth is not the same as *knowing* biblical truth. Two men were asked to recite the twenty-third Psalm. The first was a young man trained in dramatic reading. He spoke it eloquently, passionately, and with great skill, milking every phrase for its feeling and meaning. When he finished, there was enthusiastic applause. The second was an old man. He stood and began speaking from memory. He spoke haltingly at times. His diction was not always the best. He paused, not for effect but for his own tears. When he finished, there was a stunned silence. Then, finally, the audience stood and clapped for minutes—embarrassing the old gentleman. When the applause stopped, the young man arose and said, "I knew the twenty-third Psalm, but the twenty-third Psalm knew you."

Life is not a performance. The most important battles are fought where no one sees them.

In persevering, we do not persevere just to keep going. We persevere for a purpose. Without a purpose there is no reason to keep going. There is only despair.

TYPES OF PERSEVERANCE

Biblically, we find at least three types of perseverance.

Perseverance of the Saints

The first is what is theologically called the perseverance of the saints. This relates to the assurance of one's salvation. It teaches that all those who truly believe in Christ—His death for our sins and His victory in resurrection—will persevere to the end and receive eternal life.

Denominations have evolved on both sides of this argument. One side argues that we must persevere in belief and works till death to be assured of our salvation. The other believes that our salvation is assured when we receive Christ and cannot be removed. To settle this argument is beyond the scope of this work. I lean toward the second view. If you question your personal salvation, stop right here and pray to God, stating or restating your personal commitment to and belief in Jesus Christ as Savior and Lord. This is an issue of your heart, not just your mouth: "That if you confess with your mouth, 'Jesus is Lord,' and believe in your heart that God raised him from the dead, you will be saved. For it is with your heart that you believe and are justified, and it is with your mouth that you confess and are saved" (Romans 10:9-10).

Perseverance in Fruit and Good Works

The second is perseverance in terms of fruit and good works. Jesus taught about this in Matthew 13:3-9 and 18-23:

> Then he told them many things in parables, saying: "A farmer went out to sow his seed. As he was scattering the seed, some fell along the path, and the birds came and ate it up. Some fell on rocky places, where it did not have much soil. It sprang up quickly, because the soil was shallow. But when the sun came up, the plants were scorched, and they withered because they had no root. Other seed fell among thorns, which grew up and choked the plants. Still other seed fell on good soil, where it produced a crop—a hundred, sixty or thirty times what was sown. He who has ears, let him hear. . . .
>
> "Listen then to what the parable of the sower means: When anyone hears the message about the kingdom and does not understand it, the evil one comes and snatches away what was sown in his heart. This is the seed sown along the path. The one who received the seed that fell on rocky places is the man who hears the word and at once receives it with joy. But since he has no root, he lasts only a short time. When trouble or persecution comes because of the word, he quickly falls away. The one who received the seed that fell among the thorns is the man who hears the word, but the worries of this life and the deceitfulness of wealth choke it, making it unfruitful. But the one who received the seed that fell on good soil is the man who hears the word and understands it. He produces a crop, yielding a hundred, sixty or thirty times what was sown."

As with many parables, there is a debate on this one's precise interpretation. I believe the first two people in this parable are unbelievers. The first person never understands or grasps the concept. The second person quickly agrees to the gospel, apparently embraces it, but it never *took root*. Salvation never became a reality in his or her life.

The last two are believers. The third person receives the Word, but allows it to be choked by "the worries of this life and the deceitfulness of wealth." This choking prevents any fruit from appearing. The fourth person grows healthy roots and bears fruit abundantly.

Healthy believers persevere for fruitfulness. They want their lives to be used by God. They take steps to prepare for spiritual fruit. They do not make the fruit, but simply nurture the conditions in which fruit grows.

I see three varieties of biblical fruit:

1. The fruit of character. This relates to inner change and inner growth. This is what we call *the fruit of the Spirit,* described in Galatians 5:22-23. It involves our inner motivations and attitudes as well as our outward expressions that people can see. It is what we call "godly character" in a man or woman.

2. The fruit of good works. These are acts of service toward others—feeding the poor, binding up physical wounds, helping the brokenhearted, caring for orphans and widows, caring for the sick, helping the helpless, and giving of one's resources. We persevere even when we feel we cannot make a difference with our small part. We are told to "not become weary in doing good" and to "do good to all people" (Galatians 6:9,10).

3. The fruit of reaching people and helping them to faith in Christ. The act of proclaiming the gospel is central to God's purposes. This is what the Great Commission of Matthew 28:18-20 is all about. No one person ever "leads" another to faith in Christ. Some are like midwives, helping the final birth. Others quietly plant the seeds of the gospel with friends, family, and even strangers. In a famous argument about who was greater, Paul or Apollos, Paul said, "What, after all, is Apollos? And what is Paul? Only servants through whom you came to believe—as the Lord has assigned to each his task. I planted the seed, Apollos watered it, but God made it grow" (1 Corinthians 3:5-7).

Everyone has a part. *But* everyone must take responsibility for his or her part. The ultimate fruit is the rebirth of men and women—the so-called "new birth" Jesus spoke of in John 3 when he discussed the second birth with Nicodemus. Jesus taught that one had to be born not only physically but also spiritually.

Spiritual birth is no accident. It cannot be done for us by our parents or our church. It is a conscious decision we each must make. Actively helping others make this decision is central to a purposeful life. Again and again, I have observed people's lives being radically transformed as they made this commitment and began to grow spiritually.

Whether or not we ever see others come to faith through our influence, we must persevere in sharing our faith by life and word. Jesus said, "You did not choose me, but I chose you and appointed you to go and bear fruit—fruit that will last" (John 15:16). I believe that this fruit is the changed lives of people.

Perseverance When Life Is Difficult

The third type of perseverance is perseverance when life is difficult. This is the primary perseverance that relates to making peace with reality. When life becomes complicated, confused, and chaotic, even meaning and peace may not be enough to persevere. Although they help keep us going in the hard times, perseverance, properly understood and motivated, is the vital key to the power that we seek. A foundational passage is Romans 5:3-5: "We also rejoice in our sufferings, because we know that suffering produces perseverance; perseverance, character; and character, hope. And hope does not disappoint us, because God has poured out his love into our hearts by the Holy Spirit, whom he has given us."

Notice the progression:

Suffering produces perseverance. Easy times do not challenge or strengthen us. We learn perseverance in the midst of suffering. The resistance causes growth. A soft, unchallenged life leads to weakness.

Perseverance produces character. This is a simple statement of fact. It takes character to persevere, and it deepens our character to go through difficulty. This is the inner change we all need.

Character produces hope. We can survive almost anything if we have hope. Hopelessness and despair cripple our will and our ability to keep going.

Hope does not disappoint. It is rooted in God's love for us and in the Holy Spirit who lives in us. This truth provides an explanation for Paul's incredible statement, "We also rejoice in our sufferings." No one welcomes suffering—but the result makes it worthwhile.

The author of the letter of Hebrews challenges the early believers in their persecution: "So do not throw away your confidence; it will be richly rewarded. You need to persevere so that when you have done the will of God, you will receive what he has promised" (Hebrews 10:35-36). Earlier in that chapter he said, "Let us hold unswervingly to the hope we profess, for he who promised is faithful" (Hebrews 10:23). Two key ideas emerge from these verses:

✖ God is faithful because He promised to help us through difficulties.

✖ We will receive what He has promised—rewards, faithfulness, help.

Perseverance is possible only because God can give us the

ability to persevere. And He has. Perseverance is needed in a broad spectrum of difficulties:

Persecution. Persecution is a direct attack on our faith. The early believers were severely persecuted for their belief in Christ. Many were martyred. Some survived after beatings, loss of property, and constant harassment. Some experienced miraculous deliverance, as recorded in Hebrews 11, but

> others were tortured and refused to be released, so that they might gain a better resurrection. Some faced jeers and flogging, while still others were chained and put in prison. They were stoned; they were sawed in two; they were put to death by the sword. They went about in sheepskins and goatskins, destitute, persecuted and mistreated—the world was not worthy of them. (Hebrews 11:35-38)

History is filled with accounts of men and women who suffered greatly for their faith. William Tyndale was burned at the stake for translating and printing the New Testament in common language. The New Testament was printed in 1525 and he was martyred in 1536, with the cry, "Lord! Open the king of England's eyes." Jim Elliot was killed trying to bring the gospel to the Auca Indians in Ecuador. Some have estimated that there were more martyrs in the twentieth century than in all the previous centuries combined since the time of Christ. Persecution does exist today.

Recently Mary and I were in Indonesia, speaking at a Navigators conference. Eleven men and women traveled four days by boat from the city of Ambon. After they left Ambon, four of them learned their homes were burned to the ground by Muslim activists. In many countries those who are believers in Christ can never advance in their profession or hold positions of responsibility. Persecution is constant for many believers today.

Though persecution happens in the West, it is relatively rare. We live in an age where true believers are respected and can succeed in government, private industry, sports, and entertainment. We must remember that such honor and freedom is not the norm—either today or throughout history.

Tribulation. The Greek word *thelipses,* translated *tribulation* in John 16:33 ("In the world you have tribulation," NASB), means pressure. This pressure comes from many sources—from family, from health, from work. Pressure is a norm of life. We will never escape it.

Various translations of *thelipses* are *troubles, suffering, afflictions,* and *persecutions.* The constancy of pressure and affliction often puzzles believers, who feel their commitment to God should render them immune to pain and sorrow.

A character in Neil Simon's *The Play Goes On: A Memoir* says, "If you can go through life without experiencing pain, you probably haven't been born yet." The issue is not whether we will have pressure and suffering, but what we will do when it inevitably comes.

Trials and testing. Trials and testing, as I am defining them here, are specific events or seasons that are different from persecution for our faith or the incessant pressure we face in life. They are those times we all go through when we are greatly tested—the rebellion of a teen, the process of a divorce, the uncertainty of survival in our job, or an illness that challenges us physically and financially. We also encounter events that place incredible strain on us. When our son was murdered, our lives were suddenly impacted, giving

> *Consider it pure joy, my brothers, whenever you face trials of many kinds, because you know that the testing of your faith develops perseverance. Perseverance must finish its work so that you may be mature and complete, not lacking anything.*
>
> James 1:2-4

way to months and years of living in a new reality.

When Mary and I had been married for five years, everything we owned was burned in a fire. This event caused us to evaluate how attached we were to material goods. We learned that relationships were our most valued possessions. Other things could be replaced.

Some events in our lives, *in retrospect,* were more irritating and inconvenient than deeply disturbing—auto accidents, a flooded basement, or a financial setback. You have undoubtedly encountered others—going to court over a teen's speeding ticket, family arguments, being fired from a job, disappointment over a lack of promotion, a stolen wallet, an athletic competition lost.

We must avoid comparing our trials to others' so as to minimize—or maximize—them. However small they may be, they are big to us at the time.

All difficulties contribute to the process of becoming mature and learning to trust God. James, the brother of Jesus, addresses this process. The context of James's letter teaches us how to live a life of true faith in the midst of a difficult, even perverse, world. He wrote to believers who were geographically scattered (in the Diaspora). Believers in Christ suffered persecution both as Christ-followers and as Jews. His phrase "trials of many kinds" was all-encompassing.

James ties how we persevere in these trials to a test of our faith in Jesus: "Blessed is the man who perseveres under trial, because when he has stood the test, he will receive the crown of life that God has promised to those who love him" (James 1:12). Eugene Peterson paraphrased it as "the reward is life and more life" (MSG).

There is a reward in this life for perseverance. It builds our character, grounds us more deeply in our faith, witnesses of the power of Christ in our lives, and causes us to appreciate things of real value in life.

Terry Anderson, a captive during the Iran hostage crisis, wrote, "We come closer to God at our lowest moments. It's easiest to hear God when you are stripped of pride and arrogance, when you have nothing to rely on except God. It's pretty painful to get to that point, but when you do, God's there."[2]

Lucius Annaeus Seneca (4 B.C.–A.D. 65), a Stoic philosopher in Rome and author of *Moral Essays,* wrote, "The greatest man is he who chooses right with the most invincible resolution, who resists the sorest temptation from within and without, who bears the heaviest burdens cheerfully; who is calmest in storms, and most fearless under menaces and frowns; whose reliance on truth, on virtue, and on God is most unfaltering."[3]

The people we respect the most are not the successful, but those who have overcome great adversity and still kept going. We admire people like John Durham, who in 1993 at age 70 still ran the Reno, Nevada, marathon. Everyone there knew the race wasn't over until he finished, usually last.

> He crosses the finish line long after the post-race yogurt and fruit have been consumed and all the large T-shirts handed out. He has even come up on the marathon aid stations to find nothing but a couple cups of water on the side of the road, the tables folded up and all the volunteers long gone. But for Durham, none of this is disheartening because what he lacks in speed he makes up in fortitude. He trains every day and *has never dropped out of a race.* (Emphasis mine.)[4]

It is vital to our lives that we keep going in the midst of trials and tests. The untested life can lack perseverance. God calls upon us to endure. Those watching us see our endurance, not our success.

There is no joy in giving up, but there is great temptation to do so. What keeps us going, other than sheer determination? Something beyond our human will must be present.

BIBLICAL FOUNDATIONS

The theological foundations of perseverance could fill an entire book. I want to touch briefly on some core beliefs, which when studied, understood, and applied will help you navigate difficult times.

Confidence in God's Sovereignty

Do we really believe that God is sovereign over all our lives? A key Scripture is found in Romans 8:28,31-39:

> And we know that in all things God works for the good of those who love him, who have been called according to his purpose....
>
> What, then, shall we say in response to this? If God is for us, who can be against us? He who did not spare his own Son, but also gave him up for us all—how will he not also, along with him, graciously give us all things? Who will bring any charge against those whom God has chosen? It is God who justifies. Who is he that condemns? Christ Jesus, who died—more than that, who was raised to life—is at the right hand of God and is also interceding for us. Who shall separate us from the love of Christ? Shall trouble or hardship or persecution or famine or nakedness or danger or sword? As it is written: "For your sake we face death all day long; we are considered as sheep to be slaughtered." No, in all these things we are more than conquerors through him who loved us. For I am convinced that neither death nor life, neither angels nor demons, neither the present nor the future, nor any powers, neither height nor depth,

nor anything else in all creation, will be able to separate us
from the love of God that is in Christ Jesus our Lord.

As Mary and I struggled over the murder of our son, we
came face-to-face with the sovereignty of God. If God can
control all things, and is in control of all things, could He not
have prevented this? The answer we found was, "Yes, but He
chose not to do so." Mary has discussed this in her book
Harsh Grief, Gentle Hope (NavPress, 1995).

Nothing enters or impacts our lives without God's permission, knowledge, and direction. For reasons essentially
unknown to us, God has allowed evil to exist and to exert
power in the world. We are impacted daily by this evil in
every realm of life. The most significant result of sin is physical death. Along with death comes human frailty and illness.

God is sovereign over life and death: "Man's days are
determined; you [God] have decreed the number of his months
and have set limits he cannot exceed" (Job 14:5). His true salvation was not a promise of a long and trouble-free life, but a
promise of *eternal* life—a life after death in His presence.

Expressions of God's sovereignty permeate Scripture.
Read through the following Scriptures to get just a glimpse of
God's power and sovereign control:

> The LORD brings death and makes alive; he brings down
> to the grave and raises up. The LORD sends poverty and
> wealth; he humbles and he exalts. He raises the poor from
> the dust and lifts the needy from the ash heap; he seats
> them with princes and has them inherit a throne of honor.
> For the foundations of the earth are the LORD's; upon
> them he has set the world. (1 Samuel 2:6-8)

> Yours, O LORD, is the greatness and the power and the
> glory and the majesty and the splendor, for everything in

heaven and earth is yours. Yours, O LORD, is the kingdom; you are exalted as head over all. Wealth and honor come from you; you are the ruler of all things. In your hands are strength and power to exalt and give strength to all. (1 Chronicles 29:11-12)

Our God is in heaven; he does whatever pleases him. (Psalm 115:3)

Do I fully understand all these statements? No. But I deeply believe they reflect the truth of God's operation in the world. Do I like all that God brings into my life? No! But I accept it as from the hand of a loving Father whose purposes are beyond my comprehension.

By faith, I accept that God is sovereign and that He acts fully in my best interests. That truth gives me the courage to continue in confidence that He will work in my life.

Hope in All that God Is Doing

When we lose hope, we lose the very essence of being alive. We read in Romans 5:5 that "hope does not disappoint." Yet the focus of our hope must be true. Hope is not foolishness or unfounded trust.

Job, the ancient man caught between God and Satan, lost hope: "My days are swifter than a weaver's shuttle, and they come to an end without hope . . . Who can see any hope for me?" (Job 7:6; 17:15).

The psalmist sees the answer: "Show me your ways, O LORD, teach me your paths; guide me in your truth and teach me, for you are God my Savior, and my hope is in you all day long" (Psalm 25:4-5).

Hope is a fragile commodity. It relies on both fact and feeling. There are times when we lack hope even when all the facts point to great hope. The Scriptures give us hope that

> *I would have despaired unless I had believed that I would see the goodness of the LORD in the land of the living.*
> Psalm 27:13, NASB

God is in charge of our lives and is working on our behalf. Our ultimate hope is in our eternal destiny. Our temporal hope is in God's care for us day by day. We need both. We want both. Having hope only for eternal life does not always satisfy us in the present. Perhaps it should, but in our humanity we want to experience God's hope now. I believe we can.

Even in difficult times, we have hope that God is at work perfecting Himself in us and causing us to grow spiritually. Specifically, our hope is that:

- God will sustain us.
- God will deliver us.
- God will use difficulties in our lives.
- God will bring good from every situation.
- God will give us peace.

Hope makes perseverance a positive experience in our lives.

Experience of the Past

I often travel in a new city, trying to find an address. Map in hand, I attempt to plan a way to get there. Almost always, I make one or two wrong turns. If I must be there at a specific time, the tension builds. If I return a second time to that city to find the same address, it is far easier. Soon I know exactly what to do and how long it will take me.

Experience gives confidence. This is true in our walk with God—and in life. Having experienced God at work in the past, we have hope and confidence in His ability to help us now. In Deuteronomy 8 the people were encouraged to "remember how the LORD your God led you . . . " (verse 2). Our history with God is a great teacher.

A Confidence in God's Call

When we know we are living in the center of God's will, we can be confident that every circumstance is according to His plan. Paul wrote, "I know whom I have believed, and am convinced that he is able to guard what I have entrusted to him for that day" (2 Timothy 1:12). Paul also said, "I have learned the secret of being content in any and every situation" (Philippians 4:12). We need to use our times of chaos and pressure to clarify our life direction—to center on a clear purpose of life. This gives us a key reason to persevere and to fulfill what God wants us to accomplish.

Friends Who Care

We do not live in isolation. We live in the midst of people—family, coworkers, and friends. But not all of them help us persevere. In times of trouble our natural tendency is to withdraw. Rather, we need to draw close to friends. They help us keep perspective and hope. Close friendships need to be built before a crisis. Then they deepen and mature during the crisis.

> *Two are better than one, because they have a good return for their work: If one falls down, his friend can help him up. But pity the man who falls and has no one to help him up!*
>
> Ecclesiastes 4:9-10

When our son died, at least six couples immediately rushed to our aid to help and sustain us. In retrospect, I don't know how we would have made it without their love and practical help.

We need encouragement when we are down. We need love when we are lonely. We need correction when we sin. We need challenge when we are mired in self-pity. We need someone to just *be there*.

Practical Suggestions

Perseverance is not simple, even in the best of circumstances. Several things have helped me and many others endure difficult times. These suggestions are short and simple. Don't be misled by their simplicity. They are powerful and effective.

Get well. We need to be healthy physically, emotionally, and spiritually. Take the time for a physical examination. Focus on regular exercise and adequate sleep. You may need to reduce your schedule and remove some pressures. Your personal well-being should take priority.

Learn and practice basic spiritual disciplines. Daily time with God is imperative to gain spiritual strength for perseverance. There is no substitute. We know that we cannot survive without eating food and drinking water daily. Yet it is easy to neglect spiritual nutrition. Take time daily to read the Scriptures and to pray. Fifteen to thirty minutes of reading and meditation will do more for you than any other discipline. Start by reading in the gospel of John and in the Psalms. Be regular and disciplined. Try the maxim, "No Bible, no breakfast!"

In the midst of this regimen, deal with known sin in your life. Sin may be the major source of your pressure. When we do not confess and repent of sin, how can we expect God to give us strength to persevere? His first goal is to bring us to a right relationship with Him. His second goal is to help us in the issues we face.

Clarify your purpose. Go back to chapter 6 and review your meaning and purpose. Keep them central in your thinking. They will give you reason to persevere.

Decide to grow deep with God. This may be the most significant decision you make as you navigate through chaos and learn to persevere. It is so easy to skate along the surface of your spiritual life. There is no substitute for intimate, personal knowledge of God.

CHAPTER 10

PASSION

HAPPINESS LIES IN THE ABSORPTION IN SOME VOCATION WHICH SATISFIES THE SOUL.[1]

SIR WILLIAM OSLER

As I write this chapter, nearly unquenchable forest fires have engulfed much of the western United States. Each fire begins with a small ignition—a match, an unattended campfire, a lightening strike. Then it grows to a minor flame, driven outward by dryness, heat, and wind. Soon it rages, consuming thousands of acres of God's nature, claiming and reclaiming the land.

Passion is like that. It starts small. It is formed into reality with minor successes or insights. It grows in intensity to an ever-clearer goal. Soon it consumes and controls one's very existence.

Have you ever met someone who has passion? Not just a strong desire or even a remarkable skill, but someone whose passion drives them from their inner being. I am not talking about sex or lust or some perverted drive, but a real passion for life and an authentic goal. That goal, that dream consumes them so that little else matters. Food and sleep fade to a necessity as they keep pursuing that goal. All of life becomes focused on that seemingly elusive mark that fulfills the passion.

It burns so deeply within that it blurs any competing interest.

In sports—baseball, football, soccer, track—athletes strive to be better, to accomplish great feats, to be the best. In science, history reveals the stories of men and women who spent their lives in a passionate pursuit of some small discovery. Rarely did these discoveries happen by chance or casual work. Most often they involved years of painstaking labor.

Thomas Edison conducted hundreds of experiments with electricity and light, most of which failed. Galileo's relentless pursuit of truth about the universe was accomplished in the midst of great opposition. The Wright brothers failed many times at heavier-than-air flight. And history includes countless people whose work paved the way for later discoverers, inventors, and explorers—people whose names will never be known but who had the same passion.

But wait! Is it only the brilliant, the great, the talented, and the successful who embody this passion? No! Passion is not success or greatness. Passion drives us to follow a vision to the extent of our God-given abilities.

In amateur sports, athletes may never make even the high-school team—or if they do, they may not make it in college. Yet they love the game—the sport. They are passionate about it.

In science, passionate people are average plodders who love their professions. They achieve small advances, laying down a future for others to follow.

We could walk through art, literature, or music and see the same patterns—passion without brilliance, yet with deep commitment to that passion. We also see it in the skills of those who make big things happen—carpenters, plumbers, metalworkers, electricians—all who contribute to the magnificence of great architecture. Some do their work with passion; others consider it drudgery. Some mothers and fathers parent with passion while others parent reluctantly. In every sphere of life, passion is possible but by no means universal. It must be recognized, nurtured, and followed.

Passion does not always result in greatness. But passion drives a person to the peak of his or her ability.

By now you know that I love the game of handball. My skills are quite average. I have at least a moderate passion for the game. I've seen two kinds of people with passion for the game of handball. Some possess incredible talent and rise to the top. Sooner or later they slip from the top of their game. That's when true passion begins to show. One man keeps playing. The other quits. One keeps giving to the game. The other goes on to other pursuits, hopefully where his passion really lies.

I know average players who keep playing—even when they don't win. They appear on the courts even when they are injured. They play when they are tired. They just enjoy being there.

We see passion in children. Sometimes it looks like stubbornness or determination. They won't give up until they get what they want. The border between selfishness and passion is very thin for them. Teenagers develop passion for music, sports, and friends—and sometimes for self-destructive pursuits like drugs and alcohol.

Not every passion is good—or well directed. Passion can as easily be focused on evil as on good. It can be so consuming that it destroys a balanced, rational life. Passion can be crushed by disappointment. It is at once fragile and powerful.

I have seen men and women who were once passionate and excited about God and life, but later were crushed, living in despair, unmotivated. This is the despair of Solomon, who laments, "There is nothing new under the sun" (Ecclesiastes 1:9). He was brilliant but gave himself to selfish and lustful pursuits, losing his passion in the disappointments of his experiences.

I have been studying human motivation for many years. I have read self-development material that describes step-by-step how-tos for gaining both motivation and success. Often the methods are manipulative, lacking purpose, godliness, and righteousness. The roots of most motivational programs are in money, material success, and self-pleasure: "How to Be a Millionaire," "Make It Big in the Stock Market," and "The Millionaire Next Door." Books and television reflect the inner desires of much of our Western world. These suggestions fail miserably for 90 percent of people in the world, whose goal is simply to survive.

True passion is rooted in a relationship with God and is possible for every person, rich or poor. It is much to be sought after. It is not automatic or instantaneous. It is not a learned skill from psychological studies or Christian self-help books. It is not constant and unwavering. Rather, passion is implanted graciously in our inner person by God through His Word and His Spirit.

WHAT KILLS PASSION?

All of us can remember times in our lives when we possessed a driving passion for some activity or pursuit. Then, slowly, passion faded. We may find it difficult to pinpoint when our passion died. Perhaps someone discouraged our ideas and pursuits. Repeated squelching of our dreams easily discourages a pursuit of those ideals. Soon we no longer strive toward dreams of what we can become. We accept the judgment of others that we cannot do it. This is especially true of young people who dream seemingly impossible dreams, finding them squelched by "realistic" adults.

Unrelenting circumstances of life beat us down as we grow through our teen years. The death of a parent, the negative influence of peers, grinding poverty, and a host of difficult events discourage and deaden passion. The impact of drugs and alcohol is profound in destroying both person and passion. Failures early in life easily discourage young people's dreams. Failing to make an athletic team, low academic grades, and peer rejection bruise egos and dampen hopes.

As we grow to adulthood, a number of self-destructive actions undermine confidence and passion. I will alliterate them with the letter S:

Sin is the enemy of every human. Whether it is sin against God as defined in Scripture or sin against others as defined by both human opinion and Scripture, it gradually destroys the very essence of our God-given humanity. Illicit sex, lying, abusive behavior, arrogance, envy, anger, or crime toward others all corrode our inner person and, thus, our passion.

Sloth. Another word for sloth is laziness. "Laziness brings on deep sleep, and the shiftless man goes hungry" (Proverbs 19:15). Eugene Peterson expresses it well in his paraphrase of Proverbs 24:33-34 (MSG): "A nap here, a nap there, a day off here, a day off there, sit back, take it easy—do you know what comes next? Just this: You can look forward to a dirt-poor life, with poverty as your permanent houseguest!" Diligence and hard work are the opposites of laziness. A lazy man or woman will possess little passion—except a passion for leisure and idleness.

The excellent woman of Proverbs 31 "does not eat the bread of idleness" (Proverbs 31:27). Paul instructs us to "warn those who are idle" (1 Thessalonians 5:14), and in fact, "to keep away from every brother who is idle" (2 Thessalonians 3:6). He further says, "We hear that some among you are . . . doing no work at all, but acting like busybodies" (2 Thessalonians 3:11, NASB). Idleness, slothfulness, and laziness sap energy and deplete motivation.

Selfishness. Intuitively, we know that selfishness is wrong. It feeds personal greed and self-indulgence at the expense of others. The Scriptures are quite explicit in this regard: "Do nothing from selfishness or empty conceit, but with humility of mind let each of you regard one another as more important than himself" (Philippians 2:3, NASB), and "If you have bitter jealousy and selfish ambition in your heart, do not be arrogant and so lie against the truth. . . . For where jealousy and selfish ambition exist, there is disorder and every evil thing" (James 3:14,16, NASB).

Note how selfishness is connected to ambition. Ambition is an improper motivation. The effect of selfishness and self-centered pursuits not only will eventually fail, but also will destroy us internally and externally. It is a poison to any proper motivation and passion.

Shallowness is lack of depth and maturity, spiritual discernment, or self-perception. We need to grow up, not only physically but also emotionally and spiritually. Many of the events and circumstances that demotivate us need to be understood in the light of who we are and what God is doing in our lives.

Godly wisdom allows us to see beyond the circumstances to what God is doing. However, gaining this kind of wisdom requires depth in life and the Scriptures. A mature person whose life reflects depth and stability has learned how to look beyond the immediate circumstances to see purpose and direction in life. Similarly, one who has spent years probing the depth of Scripture, both understanding and applying it, sees the ultimate purpose in the turmoil of the present.

One final S is not self-induced:

Suffering. We all realize that suffering is the norm of human existence. None of us can avoid it. Yet there come times when it seems we have reached the limit of suffering, and we feel overwhelmed. This is often the result of multiple events cascading into our lives at nearly the same time. I must admit, for many months following our son's murder, I had almost no motivation and no passion for anything except survival. Prior to this I had lost a stepfather, father, stepmother, and grandmother within a period of eighteen months. My passion for life, work, and even God slowly returned after many months.

The key elements that helped me rebuild were time with God in His Word, my past grounding in Scripture, my experience at having seen God work in the past, and close friends who encouraged me. So don't be overly discouraged if suffering has driven passion from your life. With positive and deliberate work, it will return. Also, let me remind you that suffering need not be hugely tragic to affect you. It could be significantly lesser things that nonetheless affect you deeply.

THE BUILDING BLOCKS OF PASSION

No one can manufacture passion. All the self-talk and motivational hype will not do it. Passion comes from deep within the heart and soul. It goes beyond personality and even gifting. Only God can implant true passion in our lives. This passion, rooted in God, will be lasting and effective. But how does one actually receive this passion for life from God?

True biblical passion reduces to a pursuit of two major goals. From these all other passions evolve.

The first is a passion for God Himself. Some would describe this as a passion for the glory of God. The Westminster Catechism states, "The chief end of man is to glorify God, and to enjoy him forever."[2]

Simply stated, this means that our entire life energy should focus on honoring and serving God. This is a big order—not one to be taken lightly or achieved easily. One of the many statements in the Scriptures commanding such a life is 1 Corinthians 10:31: "So whatever you eat or drink or whatever you do, do it all for the glory of God."

This does not mean leaving a job and becoming a religious professional or somehow adopting a "religious" demeanor. But it does mean a deep personal commitment to love God and to obey Him in daily life.

The Greek word for glory is *doxa,* from which we get the word *doxology*. We often think of glorifying God as saying or singing praise to Him. That is good, but it is not the most important form of glorifying. The real test is that our lives reflect the glory of God in practical, tangible ways. This is what Jesus meant when He said, "Let your light shine before men in such a way that they may see your good works, and glorify your Father who is in heaven" (Matthew 5:16, NASB).

We also must decide to make a deep inner commitment to put God first in our lives. When our inner life and our external actions focus on glorifying God, real power will emanate from us.

The second foundational passion relates to the gospel of Jesus Christ. The centerpiece of God's ultimate plan, according to Scripture, is Jesus Christ. Not just Jesus the man, but Jesus the Son of God who lived the perfect life, died for the sins of all mankind, and rose again from the dead. This is the heart of the gospel. It is the "good news." But the good news is bad news to those who willingly reject the salvation offered in Jesus. The passion for the gospel is twofold. First, the gospel must be believed personally. Only by believing this gospel can one actually glorify God. The apostle Paul, writing to believers in Philippi, described Jesus like this:

> Therefore God exalted him to the highest place and gave him the name that is above every name, that at the name of Jesus every knee should bow, in heaven and on earth and under the earth, and every tongue confess that Jesus Christ is Lord, to the glory of God the Father. (Philippians 2:9-11)

Paul stated that as a result of Jesus' obedience in dying on the cross, God would ultimately cause every human being, living or dead, to submit to Him (see also Romans 14:10-12).

Second, once we have personally become believers in Jesus, our passion should focus on communicating the good news of the gospel to others by our life and words. The gospel should so grip us that it impacts our entire lives. Again, this does not imply a life of coercing or browbeating people to believe or leaving our normal life to become an evangelist. It does mean that the truth of the gospel should so revolutionize our life that talking about Jesus is the most natural thing to do: "So naturally, we proclaim Christ! We warn everyone we meet, and we teach everyone we can, all that we know about him, so that, if possible, we may bring every man up to his full maturity in Christ. That is what I am working at all the time with all the strength that God gives me." (Colossians 1:28-29, PH)

Many people who profess to believe in Jesus relegate spirituality to sporadic church attendance and a willing acknowledgement that "I'm a Christian." Yet the gospel does not really grip their hearts or penetrate their lives. It becomes a mundane fact, like age, the color of eyes, or race.

As I reflected on how to convey this elusive idea of being gripped by the gospel, I thought of the ceremony where I was given my first star as an Air Force general. It was surreal. I could hardly believe it. I couldn't help but stare at the star in the mirror.

It was a complete surprise to be selected, having never seriously considered it a possibility. But once promoted, I sensed the heavy responsibility of the rank, the gravity of knowing so many more qualified people were not promoted and that I had to live up to the expectations of the rank. Hardly a day went by when I did not think about it either pridefully or humbly. It became a controlling aspect of my life—and for the rest of my life, because it is a permanent title. In a significant way it "grips" my mind and my heart. That is how the gospel should be demonstrated in our lives—the greatest promotion and the greatest responsibility of our

lives. It should be the central element of our lives, for the rest of
our lives.

> *When purpose ignites a spirit, it generates an inexhaustible fire that burns in the heart of every unstoppable person. That fire is passion.*[3]
> Cynthia Kersey

For the believer in Jesus, these
foundations give birth to all other
passions for family, career, and
ministry to others. Purpose and
meaning feed passion with truth
and substance.

Some Practical Steps to Build True Passion

You may agree intellectually and emotionally with the building blocks identified above, yet you wonder how to proceed.
Let's examine a passage from the letter to the Corinthians to
illustrate it.

> For Christ's love compels us, because we are convinced
> that one died for all, and therefore all died. And he died
> for all, that those who live should no longer live for them-
> selves but for him who died for them and was raised
> again. So from now on we regard no one from a worldly
> point of view. Though we once regarded Christ in this way,
> we do so no longer. Therefore, if anyone is in Christ, he is
> a new creation; the old has gone, the new has come! All
> this is from God, who reconciled us to himself through
> Christ and gave us the ministry of reconciliation: that God
> was reconciling the world to himself in Christ, not count-
> ing men's sins against them. And he has committed to us
> the message of reconciliation. We are therefore Christ's
> ambassadors, as though God were making his appeal
> through us. We implore you on Christ's behalf: Be recon-
> ciled to God. God made him who had no sin to be sin for
> us, so that in him we might become the righteousness of
> God. (2 Corinthians 5:14-21)

1. Controlled by love. "For the love of Christ controls us, because we have concluded that one has died for all, therefore all have died" (verse 14, ESV). Love is one of the most powerful of human emotions. Do you remember when you first fell in love? Your mind was completely drawn to that person you loved. He or she so consumed your thoughts that you could do little else. The emotion literally controlled you.

In verse 14 Paul states that he and his friends were compelled by Christ's love. Jesus' love, which ultimately led to death on the cross, was so powerful that they were driven by it. His love was unselfish, like a mother caring for her baby. When we come to a deep understanding of what Christ did for us, it profoundly affects us. We are compelled to respond.

2. Living for Christ, not ourselves. "And he died for all, that those who live should no longer live for themselves but for him who died for them and was raised again" (verse 15). Realizing the enormity of Christ's act of love, we become forever indebted to Him. Like the mythical story of saving another's life and thus capturing his or her servitude for a lifetime, we are moved to turn control of our lives over to Jesus. In his previous letter to the Corinthians, Paul explained, "You were bought at a price. Therefore, honor God with your body" (1 Corinthians 6:20). This is an ultimate and total surrender to God.

3. Living like a new person. "Therefore, if anyone is in Christ, he is a new creation; the old has gone, the new has come!" (verse 17). With ten grandchildren, I have been able to enjoy, as only a grandparent can, the incredible growth that babies experience in their first three years. They begin as completely new creations—beautiful, helpless, and dependent on their parents' love and care. Almost daily they do something for the first time—smile, eat, focus, speak, crawl, or walk. They are unwritten books, ready to develop into unique personalities. That is the picture here. When we come to faith in Christ, we become a new person—moldable in every way. Our problem is that we already have a history that hinders our growth. We have a new life and need to live out that new life in practice. This means a new inner life and a new outer life, a new family life and a new work life.

4. God is the source. "All this is from God, who reconciled us to himself through Christ and gave us the ministry of reconciliation" (verse 18). All this is from God—Christ's love, Christ's death, new life. Whatever we have, we recognize it as all coming from God. "For who regards you as superior? And what do you have that you did not receive? And if you did receive it, why do you boast as if you did not receive it?" (1 Corinthians 4:7, NASB). Everything we have comes from God—our race, our health, our good looks (or lack thereof), our intelligence, our birth family, our talents—everything. We are stewards of what God has given and are responsible to develop it. We cannot develop something we have not been given. This simple recognition helps to remove pride and to implant thankfulness and humility.

5. We have a mission. "All this is from God, who reconciled us to himself through Christ and gave us the ministry of reconciliation: that God was reconciling the world to himself in Christ, not counting men's sins against them. And he has committed to us the message of reconciliation" (verses 18-19). We are not created merely to exist, but to fulfill a mission and purpose. In this passage, our mission is reconciliation. To reconcile means to appease, to balance, to settle an account, to exchange, to restore. This happens when a person believes in Jesus. The definition is in verse 19: "not counting men's sin against them."

God restored us to life through Christ. Then He gave us the task of helping others be reconciled and restored spiritually. That is our spiritual job, which overlays everything we do. It is not just for our pastors or religious workers. It is a mission for every person. This message (the gospel) is entrusted to us.

6. *We are ambassadors.* "We are therefore Christ's ambassadors, as though God were making his appeal through us. We implore you on Christ's behalf: Be reconciled to God" (verse 20). An ambassador never speaks or acts for himself but only on behalf of the country or person who sent him. An ambassador is sent to convey the message given by the sender. In this case, we are sent by God with a portfolio, a set of instructions to deliver to everyone we know. When we take this appointment seriously, it affects everything we do.

Paul, acting on his authority of ambassadorship, pleads with the people of Corinth to be reconciled to God. We have the same commission.

Some Thoughts on the Process

Three words express some of the human process that God uses to aid us in igniting passion: experience, enthusiasm, and energy.

Experience. Some of us only learn as we walk through life, experiencing success and difficulties. Sometimes we need to have something happen to us, to impact us, and to shake us out of our lethargy. Several examples illustrate this: the death of a teen hit by a drunk driver ignited a major movement, MADD (Mothers Against Drunk Drivers); Jim Brady, shot by former president Ronald Reagan's assailant became a passionate advocate of gun control; a wife, seeing her husband destroyed by pornography, wrote a passionate analysis of pornography, taking the fight public. Abortions have stirred many to passion on both sides of the issue.

What does God need to do in your life to ignite a fresh passion for Him and for His work in the world around us?

Enthusiasm. Although one cannot manufacture enthusiasm, I believe we can learn to think positively and be excited about life and the activities in which we are engaged. To some extent, this is a decision of our mind and will. Learn to speak positively about others; guard against a negative, critical, or cynical attitude.

Author Jack London commented on his passion:

> I'd rather be ashes than dust. I'd rather my spark go out in a burning flame than it be stifled with dry rot. I'd rather be a splendid meteor blazing across the sky, every atom in me a magnificent glow, than to be a sleepy and permanent planet. Life is to be lived, not just to exist. I shall not waste my days trying to prolong them; I will use my time![4]

Energy. Nothing happens without hard work. We must apply energy to our life, work, and chosen tasks. Three verses of Scripture help us focus on this.

From the verses in the box on the right, we learn:

✖ We work hard for God, not just ourselves.

✖ We must not be lazy in our work.

✖ We do what we do with all the energy we have.

Jim Elliot, a missionary martyred in Ecuador, said, "Wherever you are, be all there. Live to the hilt every situation you believe to be the will of God."[5]

We want to be fully there, living life to the fullest with all the strength God gives us for all the time He gives us in this life. As Churchill said, "Never give in."

> *Whatever you do, work at it with all your heart, as working for the Lord, not for men.*
> Colossians 3:23
>
> *One who is slack in his work is brother to one who destroys.*
> Proverbs 18:9
>
> *Whatever your hand finds to do, do it with all your might, for in the grave, where you are going, there is neither working nor planning nor knowledge nor wisdom.*
> Ecclesiastes 9:10

CHAPTER 11

MAKING SENSE OUT OF CHAOS

Do you remember Bruce, the millionaire from chapter 5? Let's continue his story.

Bruce finally gave up his quest for power and success. He sold his company and moved to another state to restart life with a new set of priorities. Primarily, he took time to think through his newfound faith in Christ. After three years of marriage adjustment and personal growth, he reentered the high-pressured job market.

He tested the changes he had made. Not surprisingly, he struggled more than he had expected. He found that ordering his family life with a demanding job was a continuous, hard process. The patterns of his earlier years began to resurface. But now he recognized them and dealt with them from a spiritual base.

Bruce and his wife made steady progress, though it sometimes felt like two steps forward and one step back. He found that his deeply ingrained work patterns, family background, and personality did not change easily. It was very hard work. Bruce and his wife continue to commit themselves to living as God wants them to live, in the midst of their reality. It is an emerging story.

REORDERING LIFE

I wish I could tell you that reordering your life will be easy and will be a one-time event. It is not. Rather, it is a continual process of pruning and nurturing your lifestyle.

Mary and I personally experience this pattern. Even though we made some major adjustments at the four-year point in our marriage, we find that every three or four years we have encountered another mini-crisis, forced either by events beyond our control or by our decisions, which clutter and confuse our lives and schedules.

Recently, Mary and I encountered another one of these times. Our summer and autumn travel schedule was very demanding. Then one of our daughters moved back home temporarily while her husband, an Air Force pilot, was deployed to several locations over a few months. With her came two beautiful daughters (ages four and two) *and* their 150-pound English mastiff dog!

Add to that a few other unexpected events, and our lives became overly full. In my usual manner, I kept pressing on— "Cancel something? Are you kidding?" Finally, Mary was nearly exhausted. One of our circumstances is that Mary and I are both deeply involved in the work of The Navigators—traveling, speaking, meeting with our far-flung staff around the world.

So now we are in the process of reevaluating next year's entire schedule. But Mary (along with other accountability friends) has pointed out to me that it is not simply an issue of schedule, but of focus. Our mission is clear, but how we pursue it needs constant attention. So, once again, we are working at both rethinking and being together in what we do. I must admit that it is not without conflict. I do not listen well, and I am very persuasive. Add to that my higher-than-normal capacity and a history of drivenness, and we find that it is not simple to arrive at a direction that we both are confident is right before God.

At this point, having read the earlier part of this book, you may be thinking, *Why am I listening to this guy? He hasn't got his act together yet!* My response is simple. I am battling in the trenches of real life. I have not yet arrived, nor have I retreated to a contemplative life apart from the pressures of the world. Besides, I am compelled to write with honesty and reality. I have to live with myself and with God—and with Mary! This is particularly true because I wrote an earlier book called *Honesty, Morality, and Conscience* (NavPress, 1979, 1996). That book constantly put me on the spot before my children. When catching me driving over the speed limit they would say, "Dad, remember . . . *honesty!*" So, in writing this book I am compelled to tell it like it is.

MY PERSONAL PROCESS

As I review my life, I find that there have been cycles and sequences that have led me to this juncture of my pilgrimage. I cannot say how you will experience this journey, but I have seen this pattern in many others—*except* those who refuse to deal with the hard issues. Those who do not deal with them often end up in divorce, misery, or a very incomplete or frustrated life. This was my sequence of events:

1. I had to first *recognize* that I had a problem. Admitting that life is out of control is the turning point.

2. Then I had to *admit* that the problem was mine alone and that I could not blame it on others.

3. My first response was to *quickly adjust my schedule and activity cycle* to slow the train down. This was a temporary solution. I found that I was not dealing with the fundamental motivation and issues in my life. I was treating symptoms. Yet it was a good step.

4. The activity and pressure cycle began to build again, leading to *another crisis*.

5. At some point, I realized I needed to *look more deeply* at my meaning and purpose. In so doing, I then attempted to adjust my lifestyle and that of our family accordingly.

6. As family and work circumstances evolved, I had to *reexamine my purpose and wrestle with God* more deeply on issues of my most inner being.

7. God had to bring me face-to-face with some *difficult times and suffering* to drive me deeper into dependence on His Word and on Jesus. This was not a "fun" time. Yet I found that I came out of it stronger, more persevering, and sobered.

8. Since then I have experienced a *three- to four-year cycle* of having to go back to the drawing board and *rethink* parts of my purpose and meaning. I have to do this in the reality of my family needs and my current job demands.

This process is not simple or easy, and it is never final. My experience reveals the messiness of real life. I have heard it said, "Life is what happens to you while you are making other plans." If you become frustrated at the recurrent nature of this process, just compare it to the survival of any business today. No plan lasts longer than a year. A company operating in this dynamic, changing, and chaotic world will die if it does not constantly update, review, and refine its plans. So must we in our personal lives.

OUR CONCEPTUAL FRAMEWORK

Our Context

When Mary and I set about reordering our lives recently, our first step was to describe our world and personal context. We described our chaotic world and the rapidly accelerating pace of change. We realized that new technology, communication, diminishing length of careers, demands on family, and general life pressures force us to adjust faster than our minds allow.

We discussed internal and external chaos, comparing our times to those of the past. We concluded that although we experience a multitude of new pressures, the basic realities of life have not changed much. Man has adjusted and will continue to adjust.

We concluded that there is no "magic formula" to escape. But there is a biblical pattern to follow.

A Pattern of Thinking

I suggest a pattern of thinking described in the diagram below:

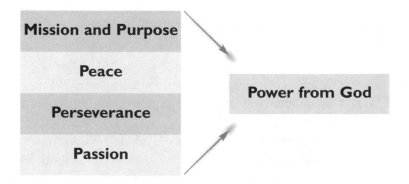

Mission and Purpose

Peace

Perseverance

Passion

Power from God

Ultimately, we want power. Though we may not describe ourselves as power-hungry, we are. We want power over our time, our circumstances, and our destiny. We want power over people, power from money, and power with God. Our desire for power becomes complicated and mixed as we attempt to sort it out spiritually.

Mary and I began the process of discussing our meaning and purpose. Then we joined that with a search for peace with God and with our family and friends. We want both inner peace and peace with people.

But all this does not come easily. Most of us quit too soon. Thus we need perseverance. We need to know how to fight through the vagaries of life and the difficulties we face when we attempt to rebuild our lives on God's principles.

Finally, we deeply want to live life with zest and passion. We don't want to just "slug it out" with dogged determination, but to experience a passion for God and life from deep within. How do I now practically go about this?

The Process for Reordering Life

We all want to see change in our lives—quickly, say, by next weekend. Sorry. That won't work. It takes years to dig this pit. It will now take some time to work our way out of it.

How long? Let me suggest a time frame of three to six months. Quick fixes do not work and they seldom last. It's like applying a Band-Aid when the wound needs stitches, or taking an aspirin when antibiotics are needed. The first decision you must make in the quest for making sense out of chaos is a commitment to take the time to do it right. Don't take shortcuts.

Self-assessment. The first step to freedom is to accurately assess yourself and your current circumstances. Take about an hour to fill out the "Self-Assessment" chart below. In the "Personal" column, include issues of health. In the "Family" column, include your extended family—issues such as parental care or children's health or conduct.

SELF-ASSESSMENT

List the ways your life and circumstances seem to be chaotic or out of control. Be quite specific.

Personal   Marriage

Family   Work

Now put a check mark by ones over which you have quite a bit of control; put an asterisk by the ones that are self-induced.

Take time to work on this. Don't rush it. You may find it difficult to sort out where checks and asterisks should go. That is because most of these chaotic situations are complicated and confusing.

During the next week, carry this list with you, adding and modifying it as you review it. Share it with your spouse or a good friend to confirm, add, or delete items.

Personal review. Having identified the pressure points of chaos in your life, it is now important to look at yourself in a broader way to ascertain your ability to respond and to make some appropriate life adjustments. Let me suggest a few ways to help you do this. Take a piece of paper and list the following questions, leaving some space for answers.

QUESTIONS FOR PERSONAL REVIEW
1. What is my spiritual condition?
2. What am I doing to develop my personal spiritual life?
3. What decisions have I made that have added significant chaos to my life?
4. What marriage or family history is now affecting me?

Again, I suggest taking some time apart so you can focus and think. Consider the following suggestions as you do so.

1. What is my spiritual condition? You need to confirm your personal relationship to Jesus Christ. Do you have assurance of your salvation? This is central to determining how you respond and rethink your life. If you are uncertain, I encourage you to pause and pray to reaffirm your commitment.

2. What am I doing to develop my personal spiritual life? Brutal honesty is needed here. This is your private assessment, not for anyone else. To do this, I find the following questions helpful:

- Are there any issues of sin in my life that I have not dealt with?
- What are my personal spiritual disciplines, such as regular reading of Scripture, prayer, Bible study, involvement with other believers in worship or study?
- What priority do spiritual issues have in my life?
- What am I doing to protect my health and personal well-being, such as exercise, nutrition, work schedule, and vacations?

3. What decisions have I made that have added significant chaos to my life? This question requires honest self-assessment. All of us make decisions, although often innocently, that bring significant chaos into life (for instance, a job change that moves the family, commitment to extra activities, or family commitments to children's extracurricular activities). In the extreme, certain past decisions, such as divorce and immorality, also need to be considered.

4. What marriage history or family history is now affecting me? All of us have a history. Our current circumstances did not spring up overnight. Many of our pressures have built up over the years, even in relationships with our own parents. In no way do I believe that you should place blame on parents or others, but simply recognize the impact of the past—such as parents' divorce, an abusive home, or longstanding conflict or tension. Consider the history of your own marriage. For instance, you may have come to belief later in life. What effect is that having on your family dynamics?

Clear the Decks!

Now, let's get to a very difficult and concrete suggestion. Cancel *everything* that you can for a period of one month. Shut off the television, don't read newspapers, magazines, or junk mail. Don't surf the Internet. Keep up your personal disciplines,

spiritually and physically. You may even want to cancel attending Bible studies and church. Don't deprive your family of
your presence or support, but do limit extra activities.

You may think of other things to eliminate from your
schedule. At first you will find yourself nervous and fidgety
without these pervasive diversions and activities. You will
soon feel and sleep better. You will find yourself with more
time to talk. Keep a notepad handy to record some of your
feelings, thoughts, and responses. This will be a "time
cleanse" of your life.

Take some time apart to think and pray. After this month
of stepping back from optional activities, we now need to take
some time to evaluate. I suggest that you set aside *two full days*
of vacation or a weekend. Don't stay around your home with
its many distractions. Find a place where you can take time to
think and reflect. Take your Bible and just a few books that
you have found stimulate your thinking spiritually (or consider
taking *The Pursuit of God* by A. W. Tozer, or *My Utmost for His
Highest* by Oswald Chambers). Spend time reading the
Scriptures, praying, and thinking. Make lots of notes. If you are
doing this as a couple (which I suggest), take plenty of time to
talk and pray together. During this time work on:

1. Your meaning and purpose.
2. A six-month plan to adjust to this meaning and purpose.

This may not be possible in one weekend away. You may
well need another. Your meaning and purpose do not need to
be perfectly or elegantly stated, but they should contain the
major elements of your life. They need not be super-spiritual,
but must include dreams that reflect your career and family.
When I worked on this evaluation during my last time away,
one goal came to the top: "Be a good grandfather—be specific, plan." I took that directly from the notes I made. It is sim-

ple and uncomplicated. Another was, "Enable Mary to find her contribution and pace for this stage of our lives."

Some of you are naturally more precise and orderly than others. There is no one formula for doing this. But whatever you do, try to be specific.

My personal purpose is brief, with a number of specific applications in practical areas of my life (personal, family, work, and ministry to others).

If this time is effective, I expect that some pruning of activities and changes will ensue. It will take you about six months to test and implement what you decide. Don't create more chaos and pressure by acting precipitously.

BEGIN PURSUING YOUR PASSION

From these times apart, you will begin to see your passion rejuvenated as you focus on what you believe God is leading you to do. Again, remember that passion includes more than just the spiritual items. It can relate to your career, your family, and other areas of your life.

Rebuild your personal encouragement and support structure. Most of us tend to be involved in so many activities that we do not experience depth in any of them. Mary and I have found the following ideas to be helpful:

✖ Team up with one other couple or individual for encouragement and friendship.

✖ Get involved in a regular Bible study where you are driven to go deeper in your own knowledge of the Scripture.

✖ Attend a weekend or weeklong conference where you will be challenged and stimulated spiritually.

✖ Include your family in your thinking.

You may need to significantly alter your lifestyle. If financial issues are a constant pressure, you may need to downsize and simplify. If work has consumed you, a change of job may be in order. If you are a two-income family, you may want to evaluate its impact on you—and whether you really need it.

I recommend two books to you for many additional, practical suggestions. Richard Swenson, M.D., has written *Margin* (NavPress, 1992) and *The Overload Syndrome* (NavPress, 1998), both of which address many issues of change and complexity. In *Margin,* Dr. Swenson outlines many specific suggestions to create margin in your life and to simplify life. In *The Overload Syndrome,* he addresses our human limitations and how to live with them. Both are intensely practical books.

An underlying idea in this book, and especially in this chapter, is that if we are too busy to hear God, we need to reorder our lives. The noise of our world and our busy lives drives out His voice. We also find that we are not looking in the right places to know what God wants. Our only true sources are the Scriptures and God Himself.

> *Come, my children, listen to me; I will teach you the fear of the LORD.*
> Psalm 34:11

> *"Give ear and come to me; hear me, that your soul may live."*
> Isaiah 55:3

> *Let the wise listen and add to their learning, and let the discerning get guidance.*
> Proverbs 1:5

CHAPTER 12

THE REST OF *THEIR* LIVES

"Hey, Son, how about a cup of coffee today?"
"Sorry, Dad, I'm really busy. Maybe next week."

The son privately thought, *Dad, where were you when I wanted to play catch, go see a movie, or just shoot a few hoops? Mom, I just remember you going to all those meetings and social events. You never seemed to have time for me. Dad, why didn't you really try to attend my basketball games?*

TRANSMITTING A LIFESTYLE TO OUR CHILDREN

These haunt us as we look to the future with our adult children. All parents know they have made many mistakes. We know how long it has taken to get our act together—in the midst of personal trials, marriage problems, and the simple pressure of putting bread on the table.

How do our children view us when they are young adults, teens, and preteens? Their view of us is skewed at best, and absolutely unreal at worst.

- They have almost no knowledge of the financial pressures we face.
- They have little understanding of the fears and hurts that we have experienced or are experiencing.
- They find the thought of parents having sex, at their advanced age, embarrassing and ludicrous.

✖ They do not know our personal purposes and inner drives.
✖ Parents have no personalities—they are just "Mom and Dad."
✖ Seeing us as anything but parents is difficult.
✖ There is little recognition that parents have a life beyond the home.

As I grew up, I had no idea what my parents thought or the fears they experienced. We had little by way of finances or material goods, but I did not really know how difficult times were for them. My mother put cash in envelopes each payday for each bill to be paid. She or my father personally carried the cash to the store or doctor or bank. I knew little of their conflicts with their parents and the pressures it put on them. I remember seeing my mother cry after an encounter with her mother-in-law, but I had no idea what was really happening.

Why should it be different with our own children? Yet we somehow want to communicate with them better and more fully than our parents did with us. We want to help them:
✖ Avoid our mistakes.
✖ Deepen their lives sooner than we did.
✖ Have a sense of personal direction from God.
✖ Have a mission, peace, and passion.
✖ Keep from being overwhelmed by the chaos and the new world in which they live.

How do we do this? If strained relationships develop, or if our children exhibit bizarre behavior or offer limited communication, we seem to be the last ones to help them. So we seek to push them to youth pastors, Young Life, Youth for Christ, or the Fellowship of Christian Athletes. When they enter college we hope they will connect with The Navigators, InterVarsity Christian Fellowship, Campus Crusade for Christ, or a good church. These sources are all good, but they can never replace the personal input of loving, godly parents.

What our children become is often a direct result of what we are and do. We impact their lives even when we do not try. They reflect us in ways beyond genetics and personality. They imitate what we do and believe. They reflect our values and they respond to chaos much the same as we do.

Do you remember our discussion of 2 Corinthians 4:7 in chapter 4? Our children definitely view us as imperfect earthen vessels—cracked pots! Do they see God doing a deep work in our lives? Do they recognize God in us?

WHAT DO WE WANT TO TRANSMIT?

I use the word *transmit* rather than *teach*. Most of what our children learn from us is transmitted through their observation of us rather than through our teaching. Therefore, we need to give serious thought to what we transmit—at any age and stage of their lives and ours.

Here are some thoughts on what we do want to transmit:

A Sense of Destiny

We must instill in our children that they are special . . . unique. No one else was created like them. They are one of a kind. We want to build up their self-esteem and personal confidence. We must stimulate and encourage them. We sometimes think this is especially true when they are small. But in their teens, when they are seeking their adult identity, they very much need our approval. When they are adults, they will want to know that we love and affirm them. Even when we cannot approve of all they do, they want our love and affirmation to the last day of our lives.

A Sense of Purpose

We must discover our own meaning and purpose so our children can see us operating out of a deep sense of God's plan for our lives. Share your purpose with them. Ask for their input. Let them into your life and thinking. If you were to ask them now what they think your purpose is, what would they say? Try it. You may be surprised.

As they share their hopes and dreams with you, listen without criticism. No matter how unrealistic they may seem at the time, try to affirm them. I have really failed in this regard in the past. I am logical and systematic. I needed to let my children dream and pursue their passions much more than I did. But it is never too late to listen and encourage.

A Sense of Love

Parents were created by God to love their children. From the moment parents hold a newborn, love floods their hearts. Love must permeate a child's growing years. The one element of life that costs no money is love. The greatest picture of love that children will see is the love between Mom and Dad. That is why divorce so damages children. They lose their understanding of what love is and means.

In reality, love can die in a marriage. But it can also be rebuilt. That's why I like Jack and Carole Mayhall's book entitled *Marriage Takes More Than Love* (NavPress, 1978). Marriage takes love—but also commitment and hard work.

Children also need to see our love for people in our community and circle of friends. When that love is rooted in Christ, it becomes even more powerful. Unselfish love was a legacy of Jesus: "By this all men will know that you are my disciples, if you love one another" (John 13:35). Give your children the legacy of love.

A Sense of Security

A small child's security rests totally in his or her parents. That sense of safety is important for a child. As they grow older, children need to know that they are secure—in their home, in your love, in their future with you. You are always their refuge, even in their adult years. Nurture that sense of security and help them provide the same when they have their families.

A Sense of Hope

One of the most tragic feelings is that of hopelessness. It is a feeling that each child, teen, or young adult will eventually experience. This despair may come from poor school performance, athletic failure, or a disappointing romance. Our children can learn that there is hope, no matter how difficult the circumstances. We can demonstrate a life with God that reflects joy and hope for the present and for the future. This is godly optimism. This is not a denial of reality, but rather a deep conviction that God is at work and will work on our behalf. That kind of hope is contagious to our children.

A Desire for Godliness

All parents wish for their children to experience happiness in life, work, and marriage. But our greatest desire is that they live a life given over to God. We want them to follow our faith. We want them to develop deep personal convictions that draw them to a life of godliness. When they see in us an example of godly living, they will have a vivid picture of what that means. We are their living examples.

How Do We Transmit These Values?

Paul's comments in 2 Corinthians 3:1-6 help us understand how to influence the lives of our children:

> Does it sound like we're patting ourselves on the back, insisting on our credentials, asserting our authority? Well, we're not. Neither do we need letters of endorsement, either to you or from you. You yourselves are all the endorsement we need. Your very lives are a letter that anyone can read by just looking at you. Christ himself

wrote it—not with ink, but with God's living Spirit; not chiseled into stone, but carved into human lives—and we publish it.

We couldn't be more sure of ourselves in this—that *you*, written by Christ himself for God, are our letter of recommendation. We wouldn't think of writing this kind of letter about ourselves. Only God can write such a letter. His letter authorizes us to help carry out this new plan of action. The plan wasn't written out with ink on paper, with pages and pages of legal footnotes, killing your spirit. It's written with Spirit on spirit, his life on our lives! (MSG)

Paul found he was having to defend himself and his ministry to his friends—and some enemies—in the ancient city of Corinth. He considers the idea of witnesses on his behalf or letters of endorsement to speak for him. He introduces the argument that the Corinthians themselves were his endorsement. He says that their changed lives are "a letter that anyone can read by just looking at you" (verse 2, MSG). He then claims that this human letter was personally authored by Christ, not with a pen, but with the "Spirit of the living God" (verse 3, NIV). He says the letter was "written . . . not on tablets of stone but on tablets of human hearts" (NIV). (*The Message* says "lives" not "hearts."). He emphasized that as all the endorsement he needed.

Now, that is exactly the same kind of letter that should be written in our lives, which our children can clearly read. In fact, I believe it is the only letter they will ever read or believe. That is the "how" of transmitting our lives.

1. They must be able to see the reality of your life in Christ. Your life must match your words. When I have talked to my nonbelieving friends and asked them what hinders people from believing in Jesus, the answer is a resounding "Hypocrisy!"

Hypocrisy means talking one way and living another. If anyone can see our hypocrisy, it is our children. As they grow older, they become more insightful and critical. They see how Mom and Dad treat them, how they treat each other, how they talk about people, and how they deal with others. Our life is an open book to our children. What do they read?

2. Our children see if we are actually growing and changing in our walk with Christ. Our spiritual growth can freeze in time. Our character and our actions must conform more and more closely to Christ. When our children see us deepening, growing, and changing, they will see the reality of our walk with God and our application of biblical truth to how we live and work.

3. When they see us working on defining and clarifying our meaning and purpose in life, it will set a pattern for them to follow. As we readily admit that we do not have it all together, they can learn to keep growing themselves.

Here are some things that you can do:

1. Grant them freedom. This means freedom to fail, freedom to grow at their own pace, freedom to be their own person apart from you. It also means allowing them to walk their own path spiritually. Regardless of how it may seem, most children, of any age, do want to please their parents. Therefore, we need to release them to be themselves.

2. Demonstrate that you believe in them. This doesn't always mean that you agree with them. Nor does it mean approving evil and wrongdoing. It does mean that we let them know that we are their biggest fans, their most ardent supporters.

One of the best examples of affirmation occurred when the renowned violinist Pinchas Zuckerman was coaching a group of advanced young students. Before an audience, each one would play a portion of music for him. He would then critique them, usually by taking up his violin and playing the same music to demonstrate how it should be done. One young student played magnificently. When the student finished, Zuckerman paused, quietly picked up his violin, and placed it under his chin. Then, ever so slowly, he set the instrument down, nodding approval, and saying by his action, "I cannot improve on that." The silent audience erupted in applause—both for the student and for the master who so graciously and dramatically gave his affirmation.

Another graphic story is told by John Trent:[1] According to a story recently making the Internet rounds, a New York teacher wanted to honor her senior high students, and she did so by telling each of them the difference their lives had made. Using a process developed by a California woman, she called the students one at a time to the front of the class. She told them specifically how they had made a difference in her life and in the lives of other students. Then she gave each of them a blue ribbon with gold letters that read, "Who I Am Makes a Difference."

Afterward, as a class project she decided to see what kind of impact this recognition might have on a community. She gave the students three ribbons each and told them to honor others in the same way they had been honored. In a week they were to report on the results.

One of the students went to a junior executive in a company, pinned the ribbon on his shirt, and told him how much he appreciated the man taking the time to help him plan his career. He gave the man the remaining two ribbons and explained, "We're doing a class project on recognition, and we'd like you to find someone to honor, give him or her one of the ribbons, and have that person give the other ribbon to someone he or she would like to honor. When you're finished, let me know what happened so I can report back to the class."

Later that day the junior executive stepped into the office of his boss, a man known for his gruffness. He told his boss how much he admired him for being a creative genius. The boss was surprised when the junior executive asked if he would accept the blue ribbon and let him pin it to the boss's coat, right above the heart. But he agreed. Then the junior executive asked, "Would you do me a favor? Would you take this extra ribbon and pass it on to someone else that you would like to honor? The young boy who first gave me the ribbons is doing a school project and wanted to keep this recognition ceremony going to find out what effect it has on the people who receive it."

That night the boss came home and sat down with his fourteen-year-old son. He said, "The most incredible thing happened to me today. I was in my office, and one of the junior executives came in and told me he admired me and gave me a blue ribbon for being a creative genius. Imagine. He thinks I'm a creative genius. Then he pinned the ribbon on my jacket, above my heart. It says, 'Who I Am Makes a Difference.' He gave me an extra ribbon and asked me to find somebody else to honor. As I was driving home, I was thinking about who I would give it to, and I thought about you. I want to honor you, Son. My days are really hectic, and when I come home, I don't pay a lot of attention to you. Sometimes I scream at you for not getting good enough grades or for leaving your room in a mess. But tonight I just want to sit here and, well, let you know that you do make a difference. Besides your mother, you are the most important person in my life. You're a great kid, and I love you!"

The boy started crying; his body started shaking. He wept uncontrollably. Finally, through his tears, he looked up and said, "I was planning to commit suicide tomorrow, Dad, because I didn't think you loved me. Now I don't need to."

Please remember, your children want to be somebody. They are works in progress just as we are, but you are their greatest cheering section. They want you to be there even when it seems they reject you.

One of the greatest gifts I have received came from my daughter Karen on Father's Day 1984. Karen was then twenty years old. In her teen years we had experienced many struggles. Academics were difficult for her because of a learning difficulty of which she was fully aware. We experienced many tensions as I tried to help her with her studies. On that Father's Day she gave me the following poem.

THE PRODIGAL DAUGHTER

Do you remember . . .
playing horse when Mom was
at school?
teaching me to skate and ride a bike?
my first riding lesson on a horse
named Clown?
laughter and fun with cadets
and friends.

Do you remember . . .
when all that began to fade
and you were faced
with a frustrated, strong-willed teenager?

Year after year . . .
you stood by and watched
as turmoil and hatred emerged,
yet you could not help.
With each attempt to reach me
I drew further within my shell.

A move to the coast . . .
the path I chose worsened.
Church, core group,
my singing group—
all a charade.

I played the part well . . .
math, frustration,
anger, arguments, tears—
You saw the pain, but could not help.

Your wisdom . . .
sent me on a journey to Bible school—
the charade continued,
frustration grew.

Parents weekend . . .
I was alone—
the pent-up pain and anger erupted
and I broke.
As always, you were there.

Could you see . . .
the healing begin?
the anger fading away?

My second year away . . .
I'm homesick—
I look to you for help and guidance.
You were always there to back me up,
to encourage, to advise,
and to listen.

I remember . . .
the times you were there
caring, loving,
hurting, praying,
always there.

I remember . . .
the many times I wanted to give you
a hug,
to say I loved you and cared.

The many tears I shed
over arguments we'd had.

I'm sorry . . .
for the pain I caused,
for the many times I turned my back
and said I did not care.
I did care . . . I do care.

I praise God!
for giving to me a very special dad,
a man I look up to for many things,
especially for letting me go
so I could find
my own way home.

Well, Dad . . .
I'm home now; my wandering is over.
May I come home?

Are you wondering . . .
what this is for?
I wanted to say
in a special way,
Thank you
for patiently praying and waiting
for me to learn.

Most of all . . .
this is to say, "I love you"
and I'm proud to be your daughter.

Now I am praying . . .
that we can be friends
as God intended us to be.

Thank you, Dad . . .
for being you.
I love you very much.

Your daughter,
Karen Amy White

Today Karen is a super mom with four beautiful children. She is following God, using her gifts of serving, singing, and opening her home in hospitality.

On reflection, I can only say I wish I had done even more. Mary and I are now getting that opportunity again with our grandchildren. We consciously try to affirm all our children and grandchildren, to encourage them and to be their cheering section.

As the young people of this millennium face the demands of cascading technology, constantly changing careers, the fast pace of life, and the ensuing chaos, they need all that we can give them by way of example and encouragement. They can then move into the future with confidence and a clear sense of direction and destiny. We can model and coach. We can learn to pattern how to live in chaos with equanimity and peace.

NOTES

CHAPTER 1: A DANGEROUS INTROSPECTION

1. *Webster's New Collegiate Dictionary* (Springfield, MA: G. & C. Merriam Company, 1976), p. 186.

CHAPTER 2: A CHAOTIC WORLD, A CHANGING WORLD

1. Quoted by Albert M. Wells Jr., *Inspiring Quotations* (Nashville, TN: Nelson, 1988), p. 87.

2. Jim Taylor and Watts Wacker, *The 500-Year Delta: What Happens After What Comes Next* (New York: HarperCollins, 1997), p. 7.

3. Taylor and Wacker.

4. Taylor and Wacker, p. 5.

5. Taylor and Wacker, pp. xiv, 16.

6. Taylor and Wacker, pp. 23-24.

7. Price Pritchett, *New Work Habits for a Radically Changing World* (Dallas, TX: Pritchett & Associates, Inc., 1996), p. 41.

8. Alonzo McDonald, *Reflections on the Millennium* (McLean, VA: The Trinity Forum, 1999), p. 21.

9. McDonald, p. 22.

10. Daryl R. Conner, *Leading at the Edge of Chaos* (New York: John Wiley & Sons, 1998), p. vi.

11. Conner.

12. Richard Swenson, *Margin* (Colorado Springs, CO: NavPress, 1992).

13. Quoted by Dan Johnson, "Living Faster and Faster," *The Futurist*, March–April 2000, p. 18.

14. Johnson, p. 19.

15. Rachel Emma Silverman, "The Future is Now," *Wall Street Journal,* January 1, 2000, R5.

16. Mary E. Leace, reformer, at the Chicago World's Fair, as quoted by Silverman.

17. Marvin Cetran and Thomas O'Toole, futurists, as quoted by Silverman.

18. Ted Gordon, futurist, as quoted by Silverman.

19. T. Baron Russell, British social scientist, as quoted by Silverman.

20. Thomas Petzinger Jr., "Meanwhile, From the Journal's Archives," *Wall Street Journal,* January 1, 2000, R5.

21. Taylor and Wacker, pp. 270-275.

22. *The Futurist,* "Outlook 2000" from the Web site.

23. George Gildner, "The Faith of the Futurist," *Wall Street Journal,* January 1,20000, R28.

24. David Gelernter, "Now that the PC Is Dead," *Wall Street Journal,* January 1, 2000, R28.

25. Mark Maremont, "We'll Be Watching You," *Wall Street Journal,* January 1, 2000, R26.

26. Alan Westin, as quoted by Maremont.

27. "The Next Millennium," *Wall Street Journal,* January 1, 2000, R28.

28. Taylor and Wacker, p. 152.

29. Taylor and Wacker, p. 157.

30. McDonald, p. 20.

Chapter 3: Interpreting Chaos—Where Does It Come From?

1. Pages 12-14 from *A Testament of Devotion* by Thomas R. Kelly. Copyright 1941 by Harper & Row Publishers, Inc. Renewed 1969 by Lois Lael Kelly Stabler. New introduction Copyright (c) 1992 by HarperCollins Publishers, Inc. Reprinted by permission of HarperCollins Publishers, Inc.

CHAPTER 4: NO MAGIC FORMULA

1. Anne Frank, with Otto Frank, Mirjam Pressler, and Susan Massotty, *The Diary of a Young Girl* (New York: Bantam, 1997).
2. *Encyclopedia of 15,000 Illustrations*, www.iexalt.com.
3. Rachel Emma Silverman, "The Future Is Now," *Wall Street Journal*, January 1, 2000, p. R5.
4. Quoted in Silverman.
5. Quoted in Silverman.

CHAPTER 5: THE PURSUIT OF POWER

1. Quoted by Paul Lee Tan, *Encyclopedia of 15,000 Illustrations*, www.iexalt.com.
2. Quoted by Tan.
3. *Holman Bible Dictionary*, Word Search Software. Broadman-Holman, Nashville, TN, 1991.
4. *Holman Bible Dictionary*.
5. www.quoteland.com

CHAPTER 6: MEANING AND PURPOSE

1. "There's a Reason," words and music by Dan Foster. Copyright by Ron Harris Music. All rights reserved. Used by permission.
2. Paul Simon and Art Garfunkel, from "The Sounds of Silence," 1966.
3. *Webster's New Collegiate Dictionary*, 1980, s.v. "purpose."
4. G. I. Williamson, *Westminster Shorter Catechism* (Phillipsburg, NJ: Presbyterian and Reformed Publishing Co., 1970).
5. Alan Thein Durning, "Are We Happy Yet?" *The Futurist*, January–February 1993, p. 27.
6. Susan Mitchell, *American Attitudes*, The American Consumer Series (Ithaca, NY: New Strategist Publication, 1998), p. 371.
7. Quoted by Charles Swindoll, *The Tale of the Tardy Oxcart* (Nashville, TN: Word, 1998), p. 392.

8. Editorial Staff, "The Heart of the Matter," *Fast Company,* July–August 1999, p. 16.

9. Durning, p. 27.

CHAPTER 7: INTERNAL CHAOS: THE SEARCH FOR PEACE

1. Lloyd Cory, quoted in *Quote, Unquote,* Jonathan William, ed. (Berkeley, CA: Ten Speed Press, 1989), p. 332.

2. From Thomas Petzinger, "Talking About Tomorrow," *Wall Street Journal,* January 1, 2000, R51.

3. Petzinger.

4. Susan Mitchell, *American Attitudes,* The American Consumer Series (Ithaca, NY: New Strategist Publication, 1998), p. 371.

5. H. G. Wells, quoted in Charles Swindoll, *Tale of the Tardy Oxcart* (Nashville, TN: Word, 1998), p. 433.

6. Anne Morrow Lindbergh, *Gift from the Sea* (New York: Pantheon, 1991), p. 23.

7. Donald McGilchrist, private papers, 1995.

8. *Holman Bible Dictionary,* Word Search Software Broadman-Holman, Nashville, TN, 1991.

CHAPTER 8: LIVING THROUGH CHAOS

1. Quoted in www.quoteland.com.

2. Quoted in Charles Swindoll, *Tale of the Tardy Oxcart* (Nashville, TN: Word, 1998), p. 438.

3. "The Greatest Last-Place Finish Ever," *USA Today,* August 22, 2000, 4D.

4. From a biography recorded at www.hickoksports.com.

5. Malcolm Muggeridge, *A Twentieth Century Testimony* (Nashville, TN: Nelson, 1978), p. 72.

CHAPTER 9: THE FOUNDATION OF PERSEVERANCE

1. F. B. Meyer, quoted in Charles Swindoll, *Tale of the Tardy Oxcart* (Nashville, TN: Word, 1998), p. 35.

2. "Points to Ponder," *Reader's Digest,* June 1993, p. 146.

3. Quoted in *Thoughts on Leadership,* Forbes Leadership Library (Chicago: Triumph Books, 1995), p. 12.

4. *Moody Devotional,* July 1993, p. 34.

CHAPTER 10: PASSION

1. Quoted in *Bits & Pieces,* February 1977, p. 21.

2. G. I. Williamson, *Westminster Shorter Catechism* (Phillipsburg, NJ: Presbyterian and Reformed Publishing Co., 1970), p. 1.

3. Cynthia Kersey, *Unstoppable* (Napierville, IL: Sourcebooks, 1998), p. 80.

4. Quoted by Charles Swindoll, *From the Heart,* Autumn 1994, p. 3.

5. Quoted by Elizabeth Elliot, *Through Gates of Splendor* (New York: Harper & Brothers, 1957), p. 20.

CHAPTER 12: THE REST OF *THEIR* LIVES

1. John Trent, *Choosing to Live the Blessing* (Colorado Springs, CO: WaterBrook Press, 1997), pp. 170-171.

About the Author

Jerry White is the president and CEO of The Navigators and is responsible to lead the worldwide operation, with more than 3,800 staff members in the United States and in 104 other countries. Dr. White is a popular speaker at conferences, churches, and similar venues. He travels extensively internationally, coaching and mentoring national leaders of The Navigator ministries.

He earned his B.S. in electrical engineering from the University of Washington, his master's in astronautics from the Air Force Institute of Technology, and his Ph.D. in astronautics from Purdue University.

Dr. White started his Air Force career as a mission controller at Cape Kennedy in the early days of the space program. He continued to serve in various leadership responsibilities in the U.S. Air Force Reserve and retired in 1997 as a major general. He has authored several books, the most recent being *Dangers Men Face* (NavPress, 1997). He is an avid handball player, and he and his wife, Mary, are the proud grandparents of eleven grandchildren.

MORE EXTRAORDINARY BOOKS BY BEST-SELLING AUTHOR JERRY WHITE.

Dangers Men Face

Jerry White identifies five subtle dangers men face—from the loss of identity sparked by a family or career crisis to the discouraging entrapment of sexual sin—and offers strategies for safely traveling around them.
(Jerry White)

The Power of Commitment

This book offers sound biblical counsel for making lasting commitments in your spiritual life, personal disciplines, and relationships.
(Jerry White)

Honesty, Morality, and Conscience

For the person seeking to find answers to the "gray" issues of life, this book shows how the Holy Spirit, the Bible, and the conscience can lead to right decisions.
(Jerry White)

Get your copies today at your local bookstore, by visiting our website at www.navpress.com, or by calling (800) 366-7788. Ask for a FREE catalog of NavPress products. Offer #BPA.

NAVPRESS
BRINGING TRUTH TO LIFE
www.navpress.com